T0157922

HOW I LED OVER 700 PEOPLE TO CHRIST IN A YEAR

How to Lead People to the Lord Easily and Successfully

BY: JASON ROBÉRT

Edited by: Rhonda Glasscock

WESTBOW°
PRESS
A DIVISION OF THOMAS NELSON
& ZONDERVAN

Scripture quotations are from The Holy Bible, English Standard
Version® (ESV®), copyright © 2001 by Crossway, a publishing ministry
of Good News Publishers. Used by permission. All rights reserved.

WestBow Press books may be ordered through booksellers or by contacting:

WestBow Press
A Division of Thomas Nelson
1663 Liberty Drive
Bloomington, IN 47403
www.westbowpress.com
1 (866) 928-1240

Because of the dynamic nature of the Internet, any web addresses or
links contained in this book may have changed since publication and
may no longer be valid. The views expressed in this work are solely those
of the author and do not necessarily reflect the views of the publisher,
and the publisher hereby disclaims any responsibility for them.

Any people depicted in stock imagery provided by Thinkstock are
models, and such images are being used for illustrative purposes only.
Certain stock imagery © Thinkstock.

ISBN: 978-1-4908-1793-4 (sc)
ISBN: 978-1-4908-1795-8 (hc)
ISBN: 978-1-4908-1794-1 (e)

Library of Congress Control Number: 2013921715

Printed in the United States of America.

WestBow Press rev. date: 1/16/2014

Contents

Introduction vii

Chapter 1 - Salvation Stories 1

Chapter 2 - Encouragement To Share 11

Chapter 3 - Who To Share With 27

Chapter 4 - How To Evangelize 35

Chapter 5 - Rejection and Persecution 45

Chapter 6 - After-Thoughts 57

Chapter 7 - Contact Me 63

Chapter 8 - More Salvation Stories 65

Introduction

I became a Christian after my freshman year in college at
M.I.T. After that, God plugged me in to a Christian fellowship
that met every week at Harvard University, only about three
miles away from my college. While I was there, a blessed
Harvard student named Richard started discipling me
through Campus Crusade for Christ. Our weekly meetings
went really well for many weeks until he asked me the big
question: "How about we go out and you share your faith with
just one person?"

I was petrified and said, "No way! I'm not ready to do that!"
Thereafter, week after week, Richard urged me to go out and
evangelize, but I always said, "No." So my Senior year at M.I.T.
finished and I still hadn't shared my faith with anyone. My
discipleship with Richard was also officially completed.

I know what it's like to have fear of sharing the gospel. It is
a petrifying feeling until you have grown accustomed to it. So
you can grow into an evangelist as I have. If I can do it anyone
can do it.

The years went by and I finally read the book <u>More Than
A Carpenter</u>, by Josh McDowell. After reading all the proof for

the resurrection of Jesus Christ, I could not help but to tell all of my old friends about it!

None of them came to the Lord. In fact, all of them left me as a friend. I was heartbroken, but the love of Christ had consumed me by that point. I still miss some of those friends and pray for them – that God would grant them the grace and the faith to be saved.

So that was the start of my evangelistic career – utter failure. But, as I said before – the love of God was consuming me. As the prophet Jeremiah said it was like fire in my bones and I had to speak the good news of God's great salvation.

Time went by and I eventually moved to La Mirada, near Talbot Theological Seminary. One of my roommates, Peter, also had an interest in sharing the gospel. So we went out at a local Albertson's parking lot to give away Bibles and shared the gospel with anyone we met. We led about 15 people to Christ in a year. At the time, I thought that was all the salvations in the world!

Then I got a job at a Christian School in Arcadia, California, as a Advanced Placement Physics, Advanced Placement Calculus, Algebra II, Bible and P.E. teacher. The best part of my job was that it was a Chinese Christian school for wealthy Chinese students who had come over from China to go to an American high school in the hope of getting into a good American college, none of them were Christian. They gave me the Bible class and the freedom to do anything with the class I wanted. Because none of these Chinese students were Christians, I thought it ridiculous to have them study the Bible first. So our class text was <u>More Than A Carpentar</u>, in the hopes of leading some of them to Christ. Every day, their only homework assignment was to write a journal entry of what they had learned from God. Throughout the course of the year, well over half the class got saved and began crying out to Jesus.

Then a mini-revival broke out, though our class, on campus and many students got saved. It was incredible!

I eventually had to leave my job for health reasons, and I moved back to Lake Forest, California. I kept sharing the gospel and eventually I had to make a decision. Was I going to become a Statistician or an Evangelist. I was torn by this decision. The job of a Statistician offers far more money than that of an evangelist and I love mathematics. But my passion in life was evangelism.

So one night before going to sleep, I prayed, "Dear Jesus, I don't know what to do with my career. Please give me wisdom!"

That night I had a dream. In the dream, I was standing in the midst of the 12 Apostles in the temple in Jerusalem and Jesus was standing in the middle. He turned to me and said, "Follow your heart." I quickly woke up and knew what I had to do. My heart's desire was for evangelism, so I had to become a full-time evangelist! I knew God would be with me!

So I founded a 501-C3 Non-Profit Organization and named it Salvation United. During the first few months I led a few people to the Lord and felt great about it. But as time went by, God gave me the idea of sharing the gospel with high school students. That was when the number of decisions for Christ exploded. Every day, I would go to a high school campus while they were getting off of school and lead students to the Lord using my gospel tract (shared later in the book) while standing on a public street where it is legal because of our freedom of speech. The rest is history. Over the next year, I lead over 700 students to the Lord and had great joy in the Holy Spirit in my work! I can't believe that God has both given me and allowed me to use the desire of my heart as a career path.

During this time, I began discipling another man, named Brian, and he started to lead others to Christ by himself. It was so rewarding and our method so easy, I wanted to write this book to fellow evangelists in the body of Christ to let them know that what I have done they can also do.

God is with you in evangelism and it is His glorious will to save and disciple the lost! If you read this book, you will be encouraged, edified, instructed on method and prepared for the persecution and rejection that naturally happen when you share the good news.

I'd like to start out with a few stories of the harvest that I have seen over the past year. So please read the next chapter to enjoy the stories.

CHAPTER 1

Salvation Stories

The following are just a few of the stories from my ministry of people who have entered the kingdom of God through faith and God's grace this past year. They are meant to be an encouragement to you. Get excited! Because, what I have done, you can do also!

Hardened Man Accepts The Lord

I was going door to door and I came to a man's home that is in his early 40's named Rudy. I asked him if he was a Christian and he replied, "I'm not religious!" I said, "Have you heard of John 3:16?" He said he had. I didn't have a "God Loves You" card handy to I just repeated from memory: "For God so loved the world that He gave His only begotten Son that whoever believes in Him should not perish but have everlasting life. For God did not send His Son into the world to condemn the world but in order that the world might be saved through Him. He who believes is not condemned but who does not believe is condemned already for he has not believed in the name of the only begotten Son of God," I said. Then I said, "If you don't believe you've already been condemned, but that's not what God wants. He sent His Son into the world to save you, give you joy, peace and relationship with Him. Is that what you want?" The man then hung his head and said, "Yes." "Then pray with me," I said. And he prayed to repent of his sins and invited Jesus Christ to be the Lord and Savior of his life. After that I encouraged him to find a good church. "I will," he said. And we departed rejoicing. I then went to my car and picked up a Bible and list of good gospel churches in Orange County and went back to his house. "I have a gift for you," I said. And I gave him the Bible and list of churches. "Thank you! This will help!" he said. And I left him again rejoicing in God's work in his life. I left thinking, "there is joy in heaven over one sinner who repents." What a blessed day!

Two Ex-Convicts Get Saved And Delivered In Huntington Beach

I was evangelizing with Robert, and I went strait to this fully tattooed man and his girlfriend. Their names are Victor and Alexis. It turns out that Victor had just been released from prison three weeks ago and Alexis had been in and out of jail since she was a teen. I began by giving them two "God Loves You" cards and reading them John 3:16-18. They both said it is very hard to have faith. Then I asked if I could simply pray for them. I prayed that God would unlock their hearts and tear down the walls that separate them from Him. Alexis had once accepted Christ but had since got into drug addiction and turned her back on Him. I said, "God wants you back!" She then started crying. So I asked them if they would both pray with me to accept Jesus Christ into their hearts because He wants to enter into their lives to take away their addiction and give them joy, peace, and His presence in their lives. He wants a relationship with them. They said they would like to pray that prayer so we prayed and they accepted Jesus as their Lord, Savior and Master! Then they told Robert and me that they were tormented by 'demons' of addiction, guilt and shame. So we asked and they agreed to let us cast demons out of their lives. We laid hands on them and I said, "I command the demons of addiction, guilt and shame to come out of you in Jesus name!" I could literally feel the demons being exercised from them. They then told us that they felt better. We counseled them and invited them to church. We finally left, after an hour, with them hugging us and thanking us.

Next we prayed for a Vietnamese man to receive strength in his spirit. As we were doing this, a 28 year-old man named Miguel ran over to us who had overheard us praying. He said that God told him to come and sit down in that very location. We prayed with him for direction in his life and that he would stay on track with what the Lord was doing in his life. We counseled him for some half and hour and then invited him to church and gave him our phone numbers. It was a divine appointment! We left him with him hugging and thanking us for the direction he'd received and said that he would come to church. Hallelujah! Praise Jesus!

Door-To-Door Ministry Leads To Salvations

I went out door-to-door in Mission Viejo passing out "God Loves You" cards. I immediately ran across a young man named Eric. I asked if I could read him John 3:16-18 and he said, "Yes." Then I explained the Good News of God's salvation and rescue from condemnation and hell. I told him that God wants to have a relationship with him filled with love, joy, peace and the presence of the Holy Spirit. He said he wanted that for himself! So we prayed right there on his patio for Jesus to be his Lord and Savior and he repented of all his sins. Then I gave him a Bible and list of churches to check out. He was very excited to receive the Bible! I told him to read the book of John to learn more about Jesus. I also got his phone number and have been texting him and inviting him to my church in two weeks. He says he will go! Next, I met a youth named Salome. She was with her Grandma, who was already a Christian. Salome explained that she didn't know very much about Jesus. So I explained the Gospel to her and told her that God and Jesus are always here, ready to answer her prayers. She said she wanted a relationship with Jesus Christ! So we grabbed hands and prayed to invite Jesus Christ into her heart to be her Lord, Savior, God, and King. Her Grandma was watching with a big smile on her face this entire time. Then I showed her the card and told her, "Don't ever forget that God loves you!" With that I left with the excitement that another soul had come into the kingdom!

A Very Special Night

It was a very special night for me. I took a friend of mine named Rico down to Laguna Beach to walk on the seashore. I'd been praying for his salvation for months! As we were going, I shared with him how God wants us to love Him with all of our heart, mind, soul and strength. I told him that I've been trying to love the Lord with all my strength lately and it's a really hard task. But God gives me the grace to attempt it. Later, as we were walking on the beach, he asked me why I became a

Christian. I then related to him my entire Christian testimony. Then I asked him, "What is standing between you and making the decision to follow Jesus Christ for the rest of your life?" He said, "Nothing." Then I said, "Well, you can give your life to the Lord tonight if you want." He said, "Well, how would I do that?" I said, "You can say a simple prayer with me." He said, "Ok, I'd like that." So he followed me in a prayer and invited Jesus Christ into his life as Lord and Savior. He then asked me if I'd baptize him. So I said I would baptize him the next day. The night's walk was filled with the loving glory of our great God! After it was over and I had driven Rico home, I praised God at the top of my lungs! What an answer to months of prayer this was!

Mild Persecution in Alaska

I was passing out "God Loves You" cards with a picture of Jesus hanging on the cross while vacationing in Sitka, Alaska. I came up to a single woman and said, "Would you like a card?" She looked at the card and saw Jesus hanging on the cross together with the worlds "God Loves You" on it. She immediately hardened her face and yelled at me: "Get the F-word away from me! And don't come near me again!" I was in a little shock so I quickly said, "Ok," and turned to walk away. Looking back on the experience, I recall the verse from Matthew 5 that exhorts us, "Blessed are you when other revile you and persecute you and utter all kinds of evil against you falsely on my account. Rejoice and be glad, for your reward is great in heaven, for so they persecuted the prophets who were before you." The Holy Spirit allowed me to experience an inner sense of joy as a result of this experience and I knew she was really persecuting Jesus, not me. I feel sorry for the poor woman walking in enmity with Christ Jesus.

Mild Persecution In The Midst Of A Great Harvest

I was at El Toro High School handing out "Are You Going To Heaven?" tracts and eight student made decisions for Christ! Their names are: Diana, Aza, Travis, Arata, Dylan, Jesus, Hector and Sharre. But the biggest thing that happened was that I was verbally persecuted by one student. I went up to him and gave him a tract. He immediately said, "I'm going to hell!" So I said, "Come on, you don't wanna go there." He said, "There's a reason why Jesus died!" I said, "Yes, he died for your sins." Then he got really angry and exclaimed, "He died for MY sins!?" I said, "Yes, He did." Then he yelled at me right in front of probably 10 other students, "F-word you! And F-word you for trying to get me to believe in F-word-ing Jesus Christ!" I said, "Ok, you have a good day," and I left him on the corner and began sharing with other students. The Holy Spirit later prompted me from Matthew 5:44-45: "But I say to you, love your enemies and pray for those who persecute you so that you may be sons of your Father who is in Heaven." So, "I pray that he may experience Your love and peace and compassion and come to a saving knowledge of Jesus Christ. Rescue his soul from the fire of the pit and be merciful in delivering him. Please let him know what it is to be loved. In Jesus name, Amen." It is times like these that I think Satan is trying to discourage me from the abundant harvest of high school students. I pity that young man who yelled at me today, but thank God for the fruit and joy of eight other souls making decisions for Jesus Christ!!!

Former Muslim, Ali, Prays To Receive Christ

I got in a gospel conversation with a former Muslim man from Iran named Ali. We talked about Islam and he said it was a religion of death. Then we spoke about how good Jesus was. But the man said, "If I go back to Iran then they will kill me for becoming a Christian." So we talked more about the grace and goodness of Jesus. Then the man prayed with me to accept Jesus as his Savior: "Dear Jesus, I accept you as my Lord and Savior. Please forgive me of my sins. And please give me the Holy Spirit. Amen." After we prayed, Bob gave me a Bible to give Ali. Ali gladly accepted it and said he would read the entire gospel of John and pray on his bed tonight to Jesus Christ. Praise God! Then he went next door and bought me a pizza from B.J.'s for lunch to show his appreciation. God is so good!

Three Get Saved At Seal Beach

I went to Seal Beach and passed out "Jesus Loves You" cards with my friend Brian. First, we met a Buddhist father and daughter. I shared the love of God with them and that they are already condemned if they don't believe in Jesus. But that's not what God wants! He sent His Son into the world not to condemn the world but to save it. The daughter, Mia, accepted the word and said she wanted to become a Christian. So, with no resistance from her father, I lead her in a prayer to put off her sins and accept Jesus Christ as her Lord and Savior. And so she received the gift of the Holy Spirit. She was so excited! I gave her a Bible and told her to read the gospel of John. Brian and I rejoiced that a Buddhist just got saved! Then, Brian passed out a card to a couple with names Chris and Mitzy. They accepted the gospel with awe in their eyes and they each prayed to receive Jesus Christ as their Lord and Savior. I, then, gave them each Bibles and told them to read the gospel of John. Chris said, "Thank you! Thank you!" As we parted ways, I congratulated Brian on leading two people to Christ. It was a great day!!!

Michael Asks Many Questions And Then Gives His Life To The Lord

I was out doing evangelism at Trabuco Hill High School, handing out my gospel tract, and eight students made decisions for Christ. Their names are Marc, Jacob, Alexis, Phil, Hailey, Nathaniel, Brianna, and Michael. When I was sharing the gospel with two young women I was interrupted by a young man named Michael. He had the gospel tract in his hand and had a question for me: "Why does the salvation prayer say to God 'take control of my life' if we have free will?" I explained to him, "Well, God gives you the freewill to choose Him but that does not limit his sovereignty over our lives. All things originated through Him and come to being by Him! So we should give our lives to Him and ask Him to make us the kind of people He wants us to be." He replied, "I have so many questions: why does God allow so much suffering and death in countries like Africa?" I explained, "Well there is such a thing as the fall of mankind and God has cursed the earth because we have chosen to live lives in disobedience to Him." That answer satisfied Michael. And I said, "But if you are willing to turn your life over to Christ and accept his sacrificial death, then He will make your life a masterpiece. That's His promise to you from Scripture." Michael said he wanted that and so bowed his head and prayed the salvation prayer with me. He turned control of his life over to Jesus Christ and promised that, by his own will, he would try to never sin again. It was so blessed when he finally made that decision! I then walked back to my car with him and gave him a Bible, a list of churches and my phone number to call me if he had any additional questions. I rejoice that he made that decision for Christ in the midst of so many questions of opposition to the ways of God and His dealings with men. It surely was a blessed day!

12 Come To Christ In Seal Beach

I went to Seal Beach with my friend Brian, passed out the "God Loves You" card, and by God's sweet grace, 12 people gave their lives to Christ. Their names are Steven, Moses, Rene, Jordan, Steve, Jay, Jonny, Sierra, Nelly, Travion, Shawene, and Shawnel. When we came up to Sierra's family I first talked with her Mom and Dad who do not attend Church but consider themselves to be Catholic. Sierra's Mom had a deep burden for Sierra's sister, Catherine, because of the bad-boy she is now dating. She thinks he is corrupting her. So I asked if we could pray for the family. So I prayed, "God, put a holy barrier between Catherine and her boyfriend. If he is not the one you have for her, I pray that you separate them. Draw her to Yourself with cords of love and mercy. Please help the family through this hard time! Please give them grace and strength to go through it with Your help. In Jesus' name I pray, amen." The Mom was so thankful as was the Dad that they shook our hands in thanksgiving. Then, I discerned that their daughter, Sierra, was unsaved. Her Father said, "She's been baptized [as a baby]." But I didn't sense the Holy Spirit in her life. So I asked her if Jesus Christ was the center of her life and she said, "No." So I preached the good news to her and she then said she wanted to accept Jesus Christ as the Lord and Savior of her life. So we prayed that she renounce her sin and make Jesus Christ the center of her life. When we were done praying, Sierra was beaming and I could tell that a change had been made. We left her family rejoicing in God's work and they couldn't stop thanking us. The rest of the people that were saved this great day were saved by Jesus Christ Himself! When I was preaching the gospel to Travion, Shawene, and Shawnel, I had a vision of Jesus Christ preaching the gospel to them though me in the midst of the Holy Spirit's power and anointing. All of them received Christ and renounced their sins with boldness in prayer. It was so powerful that the people around us on the beach heard their prayers and felt the conviction of the Holy Spirit. I could feel His awesome presence with us, giving us great boldness as we declared the Word of God! Praise the LORD! Amen!

CHAPTER 2

Encouragement To Share

The following are verses I have found in the New Testament where God encourages us to share the good news. The Bible is our ultimate instruction. So I have provided the biblical quotations and written my commentary on them for your benefit!

Acts 2:21 (ESV)

"And it shall come to pass that everyone who calls upon the name of the Lord shall be saved."

- When we go out to share the good news of the gospel, the Holy Spirit is doing His work through us to lead that person to call upon the Lord, that he/she might be saved. I first ask a person if I could give them a tract, then ask them how they would answer the BIG question: "Do You Have Eternal Life?" If they answer, "Maybe," "I don't know," or, "No," then I present the gospel to them by simply reading it to them off of my tract. At the end of my reading, I say, "And this is eternal life, that you may know Him, the only True God and Jesus Christ whom He sent." Then I ask them, "Would you like that?" If a person has gotten that far in the tract, it is then about a 50% chance that they will answer, "Yes!" to that question. If their answer is, "Yes!" then I lead them in a prayer where they "call on the name of the Lord" and are thus saved. Glory be to God! If they answer, "No," then I tell them that I respect their freedom of will to choose their own beliefs. As it is written – we should share the gospel with gentleness and respect for other people's right to choose their own beliefs.

<u>Matthew 5:14-16 (ESV)</u>

"You are the light of the world. A city set on a hill cannot be hidden. Nor do people light a lamp and put it under a basket, but on a stand, and it gives light to all in the house. In the same way, let your light shine before others, so that they may see your good works and give glory to your Father who is in heaven."

- This verse encourages us to be good role models to those around us so that we can boldly share the gospel with people we know without being condemned us as a hypocrite. We should live our lives in such a godly manner that those in our own household and our friends and acquaintances see a difference in us, so that when we share the good news with them, they will be convicted and believe the gospel.

Matthew 9:37 (ESV)

"Then He said to his disciples, 'The harvest is plentiful, but the laborers are few, therefore pray earnestly to the Lord of the harvest to send out laborers into his harvest."

- As I have found throughout my ministry, the harvest is indeed plentiful! To God's glory, He has allowed me to lead over 700 souls to a decision for Christ in this past year. I know from experience that there are literally millions of lost souls out there that hunger and thirst for the good news of salvation that we have to share with them! All we have to do is be faithful to share with them! God, as you will find, has already planted the seed inside of them to receive the good news. All we have to do is boldly proclaim the good news to them and they will get saved. In my chapter on how to share the gospel, I will teach you how to share the gospel in an easy and effective manner so that you can proclaim the good news with confidence that many will be led to the Lord and Savior, Jesus Christ!

Matthew 10:20 (ESV)

"For it is not you who speak, but the Spirit of your Father speaking through you."

- When you share the gospel with the lost, the Holy Spirit Himself is the one who is actually speaking through you to lead lost souls to the saving grace of Jesus Christ. This should give you confidence that God has anointed you to fulfill the Great Commission. The boldness, love and joy that come upon you when you go out to share the gospel come from the Holy Spirit and others can see the difference in you. God, in His eternal power, is the one who actually leads people to Christ. All we are is the faithful vessel that God uses.

Matthew 16:27 (ESV)

"For the Son of Man is going to come with his angels in the glory of his Father, and then he will repay each person according to what he has done."

- God will reward you at the resurrection of the just for your labor in sharing the gospel with others! Indeed, God takes great joy in rewarding His children for their work and labor in the gospel of Jesus Christ. I have also found that we get blessed every time that we lead someone to salvation in Jesus Christ. We, the evangelists, actually get to see the change on a person's face and countenance when he/she receives Jesus Christ as his or her Lord and Savior because God pours out the Holy Spirit into their hearts and they are eternally changed. And we have great joy as we share with the angels in Heaven at the repentance and salvation of a lost soul!

Matthew 19:25-26 (ESV)

"When the disciples heard this, they were greatly astonished, saying, 'Who then can be saved?' But Jesus looked at them and said, "With man this is impossible, but with God all things are possible."

- This is another verse that teaches us that no one can receive the salvation of God on his/her own accord. It is the Holy Spirit of Jesus that makes it possible for them to be saved. And because God is with you when you do evangelism, God actually uses you as a vessel to bring people that salvation. Salvation is by faith alone, grace alone, by Christ alone, through Scripture alone, and to God alone be the glory! It is God who wills and works with you to lead someone to salvation. And He does so powerfully and joyfully!

Matthew 28:18-20 (ESV)

"And Jesus came and said to them, 'All authority in heaven and on earth has been given to me. Go therefore and make disciples of all nations, baptizing them in the name of the Father and of the Son and of the Holy Spirit, teaching them to observe all that I have commanded you. And behold, I am with you always, to the end of the age.' "

- This verse at the end of the gospel of Matthew is known as the Great Commission. It exhorts us to share the good news because all authority and hence power has been given to Jesus Christ and He wants to use that power through you to make disciples for Him. This should give you great confidence in your sharing – knowing that it is God's grace that to lead others to salvation in Christ. We are all called to fulfill the Great Commission. But it is the evangelists who have the honor of the part of the Great Commission to "make disciples" of Jesus Christ. Evangelists are called to share the gospel with people in such a way that the Holy Spirit comes and baptizes them into the body of Christ and forever makes them disciples of Jesus. It is then our job, as evangelists, to point new believers to a church where the body of Christ can help fulfill the rest of the Great Commission: to baptize them in water in the name of the Lord Jesus and teach them everything that Christ commanded us. The Great Commission is a team effort that falls on the whole body of Christ. It is not necessarily the job of evangelists to baptize in water and teach every convert, but rather to get them saved and point them to a church where the rest of the body of Christ can help fulfill the remainder of the Great Commission.

Mark 4:26-29 (ESV)

"And He said, 'The kingdom of God is as if a man should scatter seed on the ground. He sleeps and rises night and day, and the seed sprouts and grows, he knows not how. The earth produces by itself, first the blade, then the ear, then the full grain in the ear. But when the grain is ripe, at once he puts in the sickle, because the harvest has come.' "

- The seed of the gospel has been planted in most peoples' hearts already. That seed is growing up into a plant for harvest. When the plant is ripe, He sends harvesters out into His harvest. That is you and me! So let's get out and do some harvesting!

Mark 16:15 (ESV)

"And He said to them, 'Go into all the world and proclaim the gospel to the whole creation.' "

- This is a second version of the Great Commission, written at the end of the gospel of Mark. It exhorts us to share the gospel with all who we meet because today is the day of salvation; now is the acceptable time for harvesting!

Luke 4:17-18 (ESV)

"And the scroll for the prophet Isaiah was given to him. He unrolled the scroll and found the place where it is written, 'The Spirit of the Lord is upon me, because He has anointed me to proclaim good news to the poor...'"

- Because Jesus has been anointed (empowered) to share the good news with the poor so He has commissioned us to carry His anointing as vessels of salvation to others who are poor and in need. I have found that people who live in poorer communities are actually much more receptive to the gospel because riches and the cares of this life are not as close to their hearts. So go to places that have poorer people to share the good news, carrying Christ's power to do so!

<u>Luke 4:42-44 (ESV)</u>

"And when it was day, He departed and went into a desolate place. And the people sought him, and would have kept him from leaving them, but He said to them, 'I must preach the good news of the kingdom of God to the other towns as well; for I was sent for this purpose.' "

- There are many places we should preach the gospel. I have preached the gospel in door-to-door ministry, with my friends, with my family, at a rescue mission for the homeless, with high school students, and at the beaches. For instance, when I go to a high school to preach the gospel to high school students, I stay outside the school, on public property, and preach the gospel to all the students walking home from school. I do this for as many days as is needed before I realize I have preached the gospel to most of them. Then I leave the school and go to another; just as Jesus did when He preached the gospel to a town. When ministry was finished there, He went to another town. So look for a list online of high schools in your area, find out what time they get out of school, and go preach the gospel to them!

<u>John 3:16 (ESV)</u>

"For God so loved the world, that he gave his only Son, that whoever believes in Him should not perish but have eternal life."

- This verse is one of the ones I share with everyone I preach the gospel to. It is very effective because it reveals that God loves them, does not want them to perish (or go to hell), and wants to give them eternal life (which I tell them is that they would know Him the one true God and Jesus Christ whom He sent).

John 4:35-38 (ESV)

"Do you not say, 'There are yet four months, then comes the harvest? Look, I tell you, lift up your eyes, and see that the fields are white for harvest. Already the one who reaps is receiving wages and gathering fruit for eternal life, so that sower and reaper may rejoice together. For here the saying holds true, 'One sows and another reaps.' I sent you to reap that for which you did not labor. Others have labored, and you have entered into their labor."

- For a long while, I handed out gospel tracts on a street corner with my Dad and two other evangelists in Laguna Beach, California. We only led a few people to the Lord through this ministry. But we planted hundreds of seeds each day. We were doing the work of sowing (as Jesus called it) and others were reaping the fruit we had planted. God has sent out sewers and reapers to labor so that He might have a fruitful harvest. Know that when you lead someone to the Lord, you are reaping the work of many sewers that God has sent out to sow. We should rejoice together in the Lord's harvest!

Jason Robért

John 10:9-10 (ESV)

"I am the door. If anyone enters by me, he will be saved and will go in and out and find pasture. The thief comes only to steal and kill and destroy. I came that they may have life and have it abundantly."

- We must lead people to Jesus Christ because it is His eternal will to save them! Jesus came that we might be saved and given life. This should give you great boldness in your ministry! Jesus has already done the work on the cross and anointed you to simply share that message to lost souls in need of salvation.

John 10:27-28 (ESV)

"My sheep hear my voice, and I know them, and they follow me. I give them eternal life, and they will never perish, and no one will snatch them out of my hand."

- When you share the gospel, it doesn't need to be hard. And you don't need to debate with people in order to usher them into the kingdom. In fact, in my experience, I have found that if a person is argumentative, he/she has already made up his/her mind not to accept the gospel. To those people, I just say, "Well, God bless you on your path to find Him! Have a great day!" We are simply sent to preach the good news and the sheep will naturally hear God's voice through us and respond in a positive way.

John 16:8 (ESV)

"And when He comes (the Holy Spirit), He will convict the world concerning sin and righteousness and judgment…"

- It is the Holy Spirit, not us, that convicts people of the sins in their lives and leads them to know that they need a relationship with Jesus Christ, the Savior of the whole world. We should rest in the Lord, while doing our evangelizing, knowing that it is the Holy Spirit that leads someone to repent of their sins and desire the saving grace of Jesus Christ.

Acts 1:8 (ESV)

"But you will receive power when the Holy Spirit has come upon you, and you will be my witnesses in Jerusalem and in all Judea and Samaria, and to the end of the earth."

- This verse, spoken to the Apostles by Jesus Christ, also applies to us today. We receive power when we get saved to share the message of salvation to as many people as we meet. It is this power that that Holy Spirit provides that actually leads people to salvation in Jesus Christ; not our own power or persuasiveness.

Acts 2:47 (ESV)

"…And the Lord added to their number day by day those who were being saved."

- It has been my experience that the Lord adds to our number day by day those who are being saved. In the past year, the fewest people I have led to the Lord, when I went out to do harvesting, were two. The most who came to the Lord, so far, in one day, has been 44. God wants to use you, like me, to do the work of adding to the kingdom day by day those who are being saved! If you follow the steps I propose in my chapter on how to share the gospel, I am sure the Lord will easily and successfully use you to lead others to eternal life! Great is your future in the gospel!

Acts 17:9-10 (ESV)

"And the Lord said to Paul one night in a vision, "Do not be afraid, but go on speaking and do not be silent, for I am with you..."

- When we are confronted, as I have been, with rejection and persecution for the sake of the gospel, our natural reaction is to fear those we are sharing with. But, God wants us only to fear Him. Do not fear mortal man! The enemy of salvation wants you to quit before you achieve success for the gospel. So remember that every rejection you receive while sharing the gospel is only leading you closer to someone who will accept your message! When you are rejected or persecuted for the sake of the gospel, "Go on speaking and do not be silent" for the Lord your God is with you to lead others to salvation!

<u>Romans 1:16 (ESV)</u>

"For I am not ashamed of the gospel, for it is the power of God for salvation to everyone who believes…"

- Rejection and persecution can cause the feeling of shame to bubble up for the sake of the gospel. When this happens, bless and say a quick prayer for those who have caused this shame. Then, turn your face to share the gospel with the next person. Do not give up; the salvation of many souls is right around the corner! Remember that the good news you are preaching (as I have outlined in my chapter on how to share the gospel) actually holds "the power of God for salvation to everyone who believes" your message!

<u>Romans 10:11 (ESV)</u>

"For the Scripture says, 'Everyone who believes in Him will not be put to shame.' "

- When you share the gospel, remember that you are out there to save souls from eternal punishment for sins that Jesus Christ died to forgive. And, those who accept your message, by genuine repentance and acceptance of Jesus Christ as their Lord and Savior, will escape that punishment ("being put to shame") and enter into the glories of life in Christ forevermore. You are doing an eternal work in sharing the gospel! So take it seriously!

Romans 10:13-15 (ESV)

"For 'everyone who calls on the name of the Lord will be saved.' But how are they to call on him in whom they have not believed? And how are they to believe in Him of whom they have never heard? And how are they to hear without someone preaching? And how are they to preach unless they are sent? As it is written, 'How beautiful are the feet of those who preach the good news.' "

- Remember that everyone who accepts your gospel, if it has fallen on good soil, will be saved! But people will never hear the good news of eternal life and salvation in Christ unless you go out there and tell them about it! It is God who is commissioning you to preach the gospel to the lost. It is a most high calling! And, God actually says, "How beautiful are the feet of those (yours in this case) who preach the good news."

2 Corinthians 5:20 (ESV)

"Therefore, we are ambassadors for Christ, God making his appeal through us..."

- When you go out to share the gospel, you are actually representing Christ to the lost. And this verse says that it is God who is appealing to them through you! Consider the exalted nature of your calling in Christ Jesus! He is actually sending you to do the work of saving people, through His will and power, from everlasting punishment. Whenever you lead someone to Christ, there is rejoicing in heaven because another has been added to the book of life and will share eternally in the everlasting love, joy, peace and the presence of the Holy Spirit of Jesus Christ in Heaven! Praise God for your eternal work!

2 Corinthians 6:2 (ESV)

"...Behold, now is the favorable time; behold, now is the day of salvation."

- I have often used this verse when sharing with someone who is unsure if they want to accept the gospel at the time I am delivering it. Remember to tell them that they have no certainty about tomorrow; they don't know whether they will be alive or dead. So "now is the favorable time; behold, now is the day of salvation." Today they have a chance, but tomorrow may be too late!

2 Timothy 4:5 (ESV)

"As for you, always be sober-minded, endure suffering, do the work of an evangelist, fulfill your ministry."

- The Apostle Paul wrote this in his second letter to his beloved child in the faith, Timothy. As is revealed here, Timothy was an evangelist. Paul therefore exhorts Timothy, and I exhort you, to do the work of an evangelist (go out there and get as many people saved as possible), fulfill your ministry (it has eternal rewards)!

CHAPTER 3

Who To Share With

Just as I stated in Chapter 2 (Encouragement To Share), I believe the Bible is our sole guide to truth. Below are the verses in the New Testament I could find on whom you should share the gospel with. I have exposited them (given my commentary on them) for you so that you might find the most effective places and times to share the gospel in the area surrounding where you live. So, here it is:

<u>Matthew 9:10-13 (ESV)</u>

"And as Jesus reclined at table in the house, behold, many tax collectors and sinners came and were reclining with Jesus and his disciples. And when the Pharisees saw this, they said to his disciples. 'Why does your teacher eat with tax collectors and sinners?' But when He heard it, He said, 'Those who are well have no need of a physician, but those who are sick. Go then and learn what this means, 'I desire mercy, and not sacrifice.' For I came not to call the righteous but sinners.'"

- When you share the gospel, you are looking to share it with the sinners of this world. That doesn't mean you have to have a jail or prison ministry to share the gospel, but it does mean that you are looking to share with people who recognize that they are sinners. So I look for places to share the gospel where the "everyman" goes, not at churches or religious services. I have found the most effective way of sharing the gospel in my own neighborhood, during the 9-month school year, is at public high schools, when the students are getting out of school at the end of their day, between the hours of 2:00 pm to 3:30 pm. During the summer, the schools are off. So I go to the beaches to catch all the people just sitting on the sand waiting for someone to come up to them and talk with them. In your area, you may have no beach, so I would recommend finding a place where people 1) have the time to talk and 2) are common, non-church going people. Try a park on a Saturday or Sunday or some place like that. You can find parks online and get maps of all the parks in your area. I guarantee you that there will be unsaved people there who are willing to give you the time to share the gospel. And great will be your harvest!

Matthew 11:25 (ESV)

"At that time Jesus declared, 'I thank you, Father, Lord of Heaven and earth, that you have hidden these things from the wise and understanding and revealed them to little children; yes, Father, for such was your gracious will.'"

- I have found that the youth are the most receptive to the good news. That doesn't mean you have to go to elementary schools to share the gospel. In fact, you'd meet some pretty angry parents if you did that. But you are looking for people who have a "child's heart". That means they are looking for new knowledge and understanding. The age groups I have found most effective to share with are high school students, college students and young adults; the ones who are getting out from under their parents wings and trying to figure out how faith and life work on their own. That doesn't mean I never share the gospel with the older folk or the children. In fact, I've led many adults and children to the faith. But I only share the gospel with a child if I first share it with their parents. And I sometimes share the gospel with an adult when I sense in the Spirit that they are open to hearing my message. For the most part, adults are set in their ways and beliefs already and like to argue and debate with me. I feel called to the young adults so most of the time, I am looking to share the gospel with high school, college and young adults because I have found that they are the most open to hearing the good news!

Matthew 13:53-58 (ESV)

"And when Jesus had finished these parables, He went away from there, and coming to his hometown He taught them in their synagogue, so that they were astonished, and said, 'Where did this man get this wisdom and these mighty works? Is not this the carpenter's son? Is not his mother called Mary? And are not his brothers James and Joseph, and Simon and Judas? And are not all his sisters with us? Where then did this man get all these things?' And they took offense at Him. But Jesus said to them, 'A prophet is not without honor except in his hometown and in his own household.' And He did not do many mighty works there, because of their unbelief."

- The most ineffective place that Jesus ever shared the gospel was in His hometown of Nazareth. Even his own family rejected him until he rose from the dead as a proof to them! That means the most infertile soil in your life will likely be your family and friends. As Jesus said, "A prophet (and evangelist in your case) is not without honor except in his hometown and in his own household." That doesn't mean you should never try to share the good news with your friends, acquaintances and family. I have done so and led a few to the Lord. But the greatest harvest comes when you share the gospel with people you don't know because they instantly have more respect for you. So you should primarily go to share the gospel in public places where people you don't know surround you and it is legal to do what you are doing. Your greatest harvest will be with the people who have never met you before! It was that way for Jesus Christ and it will be that way for you too!

Matthew 18:14 (ESV)

"So it is not the will of my Father who is in Heaven that one of these little ones should perish."

- Jesus is speaking here of children. He states that it is not the will of God that any one of them should perish (or go to hell). So when you have the opportunity to share with a family (remember the parents should always be present), present the gospel first to the parent and the youths will follow. I have found that if the parent is receptive to the faith, the children always accept Jesus as their Lord and Savior. It will be this way for you too! The children love hearing the good news and are the most open to the faith!

Matthew 19:13-15 (ESV)

"Then the children were brought to him that he might lay his hands on them and pray. The disciples rebuked the people, but Jesus said, "Let the little children come to me and do not hinder them, for to such belongs the kingdom of heaven.' And He laid his hands on them and went away."

- Again, Jesus talks about the children and how receptive they are to the good news. As I told you previously, I have found the greatest success with people who are of the high school, college and young adult age because, like children, they are seeking out the answers to the deepest questions in life: Why am I here? Does God exist? And, if so, does He care about me? You should look to share the gospel with the people who have faith like little children, who are seeking to develop their own belief system. That's why I suggest that you share your faith with young adults first.

Mark 6:11 (ESV)

"And if any place will not receive you and they will not listen to you, when you leave, shake off the dust that is on your feet as a testimony against them."

- This verse means that when we go to share the gospel, we should go to the most fruitful soil we can find and stay there until our ministry is finished there. When you go some place and your ministry is unfruitful, then it is probably the case that you are trying to harvest on bad soil. Remember you have to harvest where the fruit is ripe for the picking! So, if you do share the gospel unsuccessfully in some place for a period of time, don't give up on evangelism! Just give up on that spot for evangelism. Find a new spot where the people have free time and are willing to talk about things pertaining to the gospel of Jesus Christ. Public areas in poor neighborhoods are always good such as parks, the beach and public schools (while on public property, when the kids are getting off of school and have the time to talk).

Luke 18:17 (ESV)

"Truly, I say to you, whoever does not receive the kingdom of God like a child shall not enter it."

- People must receive the gospel like a little child receives truth from his/her parents. That's why you need to look for people who are hungry for answers to the deepest questions in life when you are looking to share the gospel. As I've said before, young people, who are getting out from under their parents wings and developing what they believe about life and God, are the best people to share the good news with! May your harvest be great!

CHAPTER 4

How To Evangelize

Your success and ease of sharing as an evangelist lies in three distinct areas: 1) Audience – who you choose to share with is equally as important as anything else in your success as an evangelist. As I've stated before, I have found, and research confirms, that sharing with teenagers is most effective because they have childlike faith and are developing their own belief systems. 2) Method – as I propose in the rest of this chapter, the method and the tract I use have led over 700 people to Christ in the last year. Print out copies of my tract and use them when you share. And follow all the advice in this chapter when you are sharing. This will hone and perfect your method. 3) Anointing – if you are reading this book, you obviously have some calling to evangelize. Remember that obeying God's Word to evangelize will, in fact, perfect God's love through you to the lost (1 John 2:5). It is the perfecting of Christ's love to the lost that will lead you to a greater anointing (empowerment) for evangelism. So get out there and practice sharing the gospel and God's anointing will grow on your life. These are the three components to successful and simple evangelism – choosing the right audience, using the right method, and having the right anointing. If all three of these aspects are present in your ministry, you will bear maximum fruit. And that's just what I want to see happen for you!

This chapter is broken up into five sections: 1) Finding someone to share the gospel with, 2) Prayer beforehand, 3) Evangelism, 4) Follow up, and 5) Thanksgiving. I believe all of these things need to be included in your toolbox for easy and successful soul winning!

1. Finding Someone To Share The Gospel With

Mark 6:7 (ESV)

"And He (Jesus) called the twelve and began to send them out two by two..."

- In my experience, the best, most fruitful, most joyful times doing evangelism were done with another brother or sister in Christ. Jesus Himself, as this verse indicates, sent His disciples out to preach in the nearby villages two by two. So you should definitely, and especially if you are new to evangelizing, seek someone to evangelize with you. The best way is to ask your pastor or mentor if he/she knows someone who is interested in sharing the gospel who can go out with you. Or, if you are so blessed, perhaps you already have a friend who you can ask to share the gospel with you. But, whatever the case, it is a good idea to start out by sharing the gospel with another companion. That way you can encourage one another when you get rejected or persecuted and also rejoice together when someone comes to the Lord. The best things are done in community. Only when you get more experienced, and you have no other alternative, you should go out by yourself.

2. Prayer Beforehand

Matthew 9:37 (ESV)

"Then He said to his disciples, 'The harvest is plentiful, but the laborers are few, therefore pray earnestly to the Lord of the harvest to send out laborers into his harvest."

- Billy Graham, the world evangelist, said that the most important things in effective evangelism are prayer, prayer, and prayer! Therefore, just as this verse states, we should pray for laborers to be sent out into the harvest. That means you and me (the harvesters)! So let us pray earnestly, not only that laborers are sent out into the harvest, but that we persevere and remain faithful to the ministry of that harvest, that many come to Christ through us and continue on to bear much fruit! It is also equally important to have prayer support in your ministry; someone you can tell that you are going out evangelizing at a certain place and time so that they can pray for you specifically. In my own life, my mother has been my main "prayer warrior." Every time I go out evangelizing, she is faithful to pray for me as I go out and share the gospel. She also shares my joy when I tell her of the fruit she has helped pray into existence, as it surely is the will of God to send laborers out into the harvest!

Acts 4:29, 31 (ESV)

"And now, Lord, look upon their threats and grant your servants to continue to speak your word with all boldness... And when they had prayed, the place in which they were gathered together was shaken, and they were all filled with the Holy Spirit and continued to speak the word of God with boldness."

- Each and every time I go out to do evangelism, I pray for boldness. As many times as I go out, there is always some level of fear and anxiety before I share my faith. Therefore, I always pray that I might share the gospel faithfully and with all boldness. The gospel of God should be shared with boldness, as it is the most important message in the world today!

1 Peter 3:14-16 (ESV)

"...Have no fear of them, nor be troubled, but in your hearts regard Christ the Lord as holy, always being prepared to make a defense to anyone who asks you for a reason for the hope that is in you; yet do it with gentleness and respect..."

- We should also pray that we are gentle and respect all those we share with. Often, I come across someone who already has an established belief system. Instead of arguing with them, I usually just say, "I respect your freedom to believe whatever you want and I hope that God's shows you the best way of reaching Him."

Whether I go out with a friend to do evangelism or alone, I always pray something like this: "Dear Jesus, please give us/me the strength, grace and courage to declare your gospel today with all boldness and with gentleness and respect. Please lead us/me to the right people and please lead the right people to us/me; those you have destined from the foundation of the world to inherit eternal salvation! Please go out before us/me and prepare the way! And please help many to be saved! In your name we/I pray, Amen!"

3. Evangelism

I could find no apostolic writing on a systematized approach as to how to share the gospel from Scripture. In my many years as an evangelist, I have tried many approaches. I have just started up conversations and asked people if we could discuss spiritual matters, I have printed out cards with John 3:16-18 on the back, and I have used various tracts. You may have tried an approach that I have not and that's fine. But I want to share with you the easiest and most successful way I have found to share the gospel that I have found in well over a decade of ministry as an evangelist. It is a tract that I use when I go out with my ministry partner and also when I go out alone, simply because it is the shortest, most powerful way to share the gospel I have ever found! It is a tract that a mentor of mine originally developed, but which I have greatly improvised for ease of approach and effectiveness. The tract is one quadrant of a standard piece of printing paper written on the front and on the back. Let me share it with you and then let me tell you how you can use it to lead others to Christ. I would suggest that your print out this tract and use it in your own evangelism. It has all the things a person needs to hear in a successful and quick gospel presentation. It starts on the following page.

Front Side Of Tract:

Do You Have Eternal Life?

WE RECEIVE CHRIST THROUGH FAITH

"For it is by grace you've been saved, through faith, and not of yourselves; it is the gift of God (so God wants to give you the gift of faith to believe that Jesus Christ rose from the dead for your sins), it's not a matter of works (so there's no way you can work your way to heaven or be good enough), so that no one should boast." (Ephesians 2:8-9, ESV)

Back Side Of Tract:

GOD LOVES YOU

"For God so loved the world (that means He loves you and He loves me), that He sent His only Son (to be crucified for your sins), that whoever believes in Him will not perish (or go to Hell), but have eternal life (and this is eternal life - that you may know Him, the only true God, and Jesus Christ who He sent)." (John 3:16, 17:3, ESV)

PRAYER TO GOD

"Lord Jesus, I believe that you died on the cross for my sins. I turn away from my sins. I thank You for forgiving my sins. Please give me eternal life and the gift of the Holy Spirit. In Your name I pray, Amen."

This tract is the only thing you need to lead people to know the Lord! It is so easy to use and effective in its purpose. This is how you use it: First, go up to the person and ask him/her, "Can I give you one of these?" They almost always say, "Sure." Then, ask them, "How would you answer that BIG question on the front?" If they say, "Yes," then ask them, "Through Jesus?" If their answer is, "Yes," then pat them on the back and say, "Awesome! God bless you! I'll see you there!" But if their answer is anything else, then tell them, "I have something to read to you." Similarly, if their answer is, "Maybe," "I don't know," or "No," to the question, "Do You Have Eternal Life?" Then tell them the same thing: "I have something to read to you."

Then, read them my amplified version of Ephesians 2:8-9 on the front, followed by John 3:16, 17:3 on the back. Then, after you have read, "and this is eternal life - that you may know Him, the only true God, and Jesus Christ who He sent," say in a gentle and respectful voice, "Would you like that?" The chances are, if you have gotten this far, is that they will say, "Yes!" If they say no, simply tell them, "I respect your decision and I hope you keep the tract. Have a great day!" But if they answer, "Yes!" then say, "Then pray with me! Repeat after me:" Then read the section entitled PRAYER TO GOD in small pieces and have them repeat what you are praying after you.

It's as simple as that! You can lead someone to Christ today! Simply print out some of my tracts and practice what I've said above and go out and try it! You will see the results! And the more you use the tract, the more you will get familiar with this approach and the more effective you will become. God has great things in store for you as you use and apply what I've just said! Simply try it!

4. Follow-Up

I always bring with me a backpack filled with New Testament Bibles book marked to the book of John, with a list of local churches, their locations and their websites. Then, after someone comes to Christ, I immediately say, "I have a gift for you. It's a New Testament Bible. And it's book marked to the book of John. That's the best book, in my opinion, to start out reading after you have just come to Christ. So read it for me! And it's book marked with a list of churches in your county. I strongly encourage you to look one up and attend next Sunday." If they live in your own area, then invite them to your church and give them your phone number so you can set something up and meet them at church on Sunday. Then shake their hand and welcome them into the kingdom of our great and glorious Savior! You have just done a great job!

5. Thanksgiving

Matthew 11:25 (ESV)

"At that time Jesus declared, 'I thank you, Father, Lord of heaven and earth, that you have hidden these things from the wise and understanding and revealed them to little children; yes, Father, for such was your gracious will.'"

- Here Jesus gives thanks for the harvest that God the Father had given Him. At the end of our evangelistic outings, my ministry partner and I always say a prayer of thanksgiving to God for whatever harvest He's given us that day. It goes something like this: "God in Heaven, great is your name! Thank you so much for giving us this harvest today! We pray that each and every one of the people You in your sovereignty brought into the kingdom today would be faithful to read the Bible we've given to them and attend church on Sunday. We praise you for your everlasting and eternal work! Thank you for using us, as vessels of your perfect will in salvation. We pray that each one of these people would grow and produce fruit 100-fold! In your holy name we pray, Amen!"

Your success as an evangelist is as simple as following these five, simple steps. I pray that God would use you mightily to lead many people to the Lord in this next year! Your future is great and God is with you in all of your evangelistic efforts. You are well on your way to fulfilling your part in the Great Commission! God be with you! Amen!

CHAPTER 5

Rejection and Persecution

I deal with rejection every time I go out evangelizing. It is just part of the package. Some people want the Lord in their life and others don't. But, persecution is more rare. I would say that I have been mildly persecuted four times in the last year. That included one person yelling at me and saying she was going to call the police on me if I persisted in what I was doing, one woman cursing me out, a couple of high school kids yelling at me and making fun of me in front of others, and another high school student cursing at me and cursing at Jesus Christ. But, that's as bad as it's gotten. There has been far more fruit than persecution! As I said before, by God's grace, over 700 people have given their lives to the Lord through my ministry in the last year, on a one-on-one and group basis. So the rejection and mild persecution has been well worth my labors! But, rejection and persecution affects everybody who does evangelism on a consistent basis. The Bible has much to say about what to expect and how to cope with it. Here is what I have found in Scripture on rejection and persecution:

Jason Robért

Matthew 5:10-11 (ESV)

"Blessed are those who are persecuted for righteousness' sake, for theirs is the kingdom of heaven. Blessed are you when others revile you and persecute you and utter all kinds of evil against you falsely on my account. Rejoice and be glad, for your reward is great in heaven, for so they persecuted the prophets who were before you."

- If you get persecuted for doing evangelism, God will surely bless you. Jesus says here that if you are persecuted for righteousness sake (sharing the gospel, in this case) yours will be the kingdom of heaven. And, if you are persecuted for His account (definitely in evangelism), you should rejoice, knowing that your reward is great in heaven. This principle holds true for rejection for the sake of the gospel as well. We should be rejoicing and singing praises to Jesus every time we undergo rejection for the sake of the gospel because we know that God is going to reward us handsomely in Heaven for the rejection we just encountered. So praise God when you are rejected and persecuted! It is the will of God in Christ Jesus for you. And, you will find that praise greatly cheers you up if you are experiencing the negative emotions that come from rejection and persecution.

Matthew 5:38-39 (ESV)

"You have heard it said, 'An eye for an eye and a tooth for a tooth.' But I say to you, Do not resist the one who is evil. But if anyone slaps you on the right cheek, turn to him the other also."

- When you are rejected or persecuted, you may be tempted to strike back with a blowing comment. But you must resist this urge. In fact, we should allow the person to vent their anger at us. Then, politely, say, "I respect your freedom to choose your own beliefs! God bless you and have a great day!" and go on your way to the next person.

Matthew 5:43-48 (ESV)

"You have heard it said, 'You shall love your neighbor and hate your enemy.' But I say to you, Love your enemies and pray for those who persecute you, so that you may be sons of your Father who is in heaven. For He makes His sun rise on the evil and on the good, and sends rain on the just and the unjust. For if you love those who love you, what reward do you have? Do not even the tax collectors do the same? And if you greet only your brothers, what more are you doing than others? Do not even the Gentiles do the same? You therefore must be perfect, as your heavenly Father is perfect."

- Here we are exhorted to be mature in Christ. We should actually show love toward those persecuting us and rejecting us. When I am rejected, I always say something like, "Well, God bless you! Have a great day!" And, then I turn and walk away. When I'm persecuted, and I have the chance, I usually say the same thing. After you are done doing evangelism, your heart may not be right with God because of some of the rejection and persecution you just faced. It is a great time to actually pray for those who have rejected and persecuted you. Pray that the seed you planted today sinks deep into his/her heart and they get converted and become a disciple of Jesus Christ! Pray that God shows them His everlasting love and kindness as He leads them to repentance (or anything else the Holy Spirit is leading you to pray on their behalf). You will find that the act of praying for them actually melts your heart and gives you love for the broken and lost person(s) who rejected or persecuted you. What we want is the love of God to dwell in our hearts and never a sense of bitterness or a spirit that says, "I give up! This is too hard!" There are plenty of people out there who will receive your message! So just keep on keeping on! You are doing God's work! Don't let a little rejection and persecution get in your way of spreading His holy Word of salvation to the lost!

Matthew 10:16 (ESV)

"Behold, I am sending you out as sheep in the midst of wolves, so be wise as serpents and innocent as doves."

- When you are sent out by God to do evangelism, you are going out among people of all kinds. There will be wolves; people who desire to reject and persecute you. So you need to be wise as a serpent. As I have said before, do not answer a persecutor according to the words he/she is spewing at you. Just say something like, "I'm sorry you feel that way. God bless you!" and then walk away. Do not get into a verbal debate with them or try to answer them according to their folly. Just be respectful and gentle with them. Bless them, thank them for their time and then just walk away. You are a follower of Christ. That's why you have to answer persecutors according to wisdom. Do not let them continue to insult you for a long time. Just bless them and walk away. And when someone rejects your message, as they most certainly will, just say, "I respect your freedom to choose what to believe! Please keep the tract" and then just walk away. There are plenty of people out there who will respond positively to your message so don't let the negative people discourage you. That is what the enemy wants – to discourage you into not evangelizing. But you must be strong and wise. Follow my advice and just move on to the next person.

<u>Matthew 10:23 (ESV)</u>

"If they persecute you in one town, flee to the next..."

- If you ever choose a place to evangelize where say 25 people in a row reject your message and some even persecute you, then you are on unfruitful soil. You need to find the place of good fruit, where you can harvest without too much opposition. That's the way it is for me at the high schools and at the beach. Sure, there are people that reject my message. And, every couple of months, I get mildly persecuted. But for the most part, people receive my message with gladness of heart. You need to find a "town" or place where the fish are biting, where people are open to your message. When you find that, you will be very blessed in your sharing. So if they are against your message in one place, flee to the next place. Find the place that is most fruitful and boldly, respectfully and gently share the gospel there!

Matthew 16:24 (ESV)

"Then Jesus told his disciples, 'If anyone would come after me, let him deny himself and take up his cross and follow me.'"

- There is definitely an aspect of picking up your cross and following Jesus when you are actively involved in evangelism. You will have to deal with rejection and persecution when you share your faith actively. So remember to pick up your cross and follow Jesus into the fruitful harvest. You may start out by just leading one person to Christ per day, while dealing with rejection and persecution. But remember that the harvest is plentiful. If you persevere and keep sharing your faith, there will be an increasingly great harvest for you. And you will learn what it means to bear the cross of Christ. When you bear the cross of Christ, you will also be given the resurrection power of eternal life. For, if you die with Christ, you will certainly live with Him. For, only He raises the dead to life indestructible, incorruptible, eternal and everlasting! Great things are in store for you!

Luke 6:22-23 (ESV)

"Blessed are you when people hate you and when they exclude you and revile you and spurn your name as evil, on account of the Son of Man! Rejoice in that day, and leap for joy, for behold, your reward is great in heaven; for so their fathers did to the prophets."

- If you share the gospel with your friends and family, there will be certain people who end up hating you, excluding you and reviling you. That's all the price of advancing the kingdom of God. When I started off in evangelism, I shared the gospel in a very bold way with all my friends and family. I ended up loosing many friends and being excluded from events that I would have been formerly invited to. They spurned my name as evil. But, God, in His eternal and overflowing love, has replaced them with friends who are very compassionate, understanding, loving and righteous. Remember that whatever you lose for Christ will be replaced by something far better because all things work together for the good of those who love God and are called according to His purpose (Romans 8:28). And, also, as Jesus said, you are storing up for yourself treasure in heaven when people treat you shamefully on account of the gospel. So, rejoice, if you are persecuted in this way. Great is your reward in heaven!

Luke 9:62 (ESV)

"Jesus said to them, 'No one who puts his hand to the plow and looks back is fit for the kingdom of God.'"

- This is a call to patient endurance and zeal for the kingdom of God. When you preach the gospel, you will be tempted to look back on your life and say, "Why were the old times so much easier than these days?" You will be tempted to give up your gospel ministry. But you must patiently endure this hardship. Take hold of God's command to go out and share the good news and you will end up with a blessing overflowing and full of glory! So don't look back after you have started sharing the gospel and desire the ease of a quiet life where you never have to endure hardship for the sake of Christ. Keep going. Great is your reward in heaven and in this life if you are faithful to endure and keep on preaching the good news!

<u>Luke 10:16 (ESV)</u>

"The one who hears you hears Me, and the one who rejects you rejects Me, and the one who rejects Me rejects Him who sent Me."

- I always tell my ministry partners that when they are rejected, that the people aren't really rejecting them, but Christ and therefore God Himself. Don't take rejection personally. They are really rejecting Christ and God, not you. And when they listen to you, they are really listening to Christ and God. You are God's representative and ambassador so, whether you are rejected or accepted, you do so on behalf of Christ.

John 3:16 (ESV)

"For God so loved the world, that He sent His only Son, that whoever believes in Him may not perish but have everlasting life."

- The Lord revealed to me after a long season of suffering that His love was never so greatly displayed for the Son than when He sent Him to the cross. And the Son's love was never so displayed towards the Father than when He went willingly to the cross. The cross wasn't just an act of love for our benefit but actually a love relationship between the Father and the Son. And God never so displays His love for us than when He sends us suffering, knowing that the outcome will be glory, eternal life and the advance of the kingdom of God. And our love is never so displayed for the Father than when we, with praise and thanksgiving, go through our suffering on His behalf because of the joy set before us. So if you are persecuted or rejected on Christ's behalf for sharing the gospel, it is actually an act of the greatest kind of love towards God to go through it while praising God for it. God will surely raise you up and give you more of the Holy Spirit's presence in your life than ever before. There is no blessing so great as suffering because of its rewards in the end. I know that's hard to hear and we often don't want to hear it when we are going through it, but when we are raised back up in the end, we understand how it was God's greatest wisdom in our lives.

John 15:20 (ESV)

"…If they persecuted me, they will also persecute you…"

- If Christ Jesus was persecuted, we surely shall be persecuted and rejected for His namesake. But take heart, for He has overcome the world! So don't give up on your calling to share the good news as some do. But be strong and persevering so that you may endure and do the good work of an evangelist, thereby fulfilling your calling.

2 Timothy 3:12 (ESV)

"Indeed, all who desire to live a godly life in Christ Jesus will be persecuted…"

- It doesn't matter what kind of godly life you lead, whether as an evangelist or something else, you will be persecuted because you are standing up for the truth of the gospel and many don't want to hear what you have to say. On the other hand, you will have fellowship with the church in the midst of your persecution. Those who are in the church will comfort you when you tell them of what you are enduring for the sake of godliness. Indeed, if we are not being persecuted for our lives in Christ, we are probably not standing up for righteousness and Jesus' name!

<u>1 Peter 4:14 (ESV)</u>

"If you are insulted for the name of Christ, you are blessed, because the Spirit of glory and of God rests upon you."

- Here is a blessing for you who are insulted, persecuted and rejected for the name of Jesus Christ! If you are insulted for His name, know that "the Spirit of glory and of God rests upon you!" So, you will be blessed in this life and in the next if you are insulted for the name of Christ Jesus.

CHAPTER 6

After-Thoughts

There are many thoughts that go through your mind after you have done a successful day's worth of evangelism. How many were truly saved? Was God pleased with my work today? Just to name a couple. Here are some verses that have helped me in my after thoughts after a day of evangelism:

Luke 15:7 (ESV)

"Just so, I tell you, there will be more joy in heaven over one sinner who repents than over ninety-nine righteous persons who need no repentance."

- There is joy in heaven over your work as an evangelist each time you lead a sinner to repentance and eternal life. Know that God rejoices over you for leading people to the Lord Jesus! Never be dismayed in your work, even if you don't lead anyone to Christ when you go out. You will surely lead people to Christ over time. And, whenever you go out, you are glorifying God because you are fulfilling his commandment to go and make disciples of Jesus Christ. Know for certain that God is deeply pleased with your work and knows how hard it can be. He rejoices with you each time you lead someone to Christ through the power of the Holy Spirit, according to His plan destined from the foundation of time.

John 1:12-13 (ESV)

"But to all who did receive him, who believed in his name, He gave the right to become children of God, who were born, not of blood nor of the will of the flesh nor of the will of man, but of God."

- When I began going out and seeing great harvests, I said to myself, "This is too easy... How many of these people are really being saved?" But God showed me through the holy Scripture that whosoever received Him and believed in His name, He wrote in the Lamb's book of life for all eternity. You can rejoice that many are entering eternal life because of your work!

John 6:37 (ESV)

"All that the Father gives me will come to me, and whoever comes to me I will never cast out."

- When you leave the people who get saved, after giving them a Bible and list of churches to attend, exhorting them to read the Bible and go to church, know that they are now in God's powerful hands. God will lead them to Scripture and to a church if they truly get saved. All who have come to Him will by no means cast out. They are secure in Christ forever and ever!

Romans 10:6-7 (ESV)

"But the righteousness based on faith says, 'Do not say in your heart, 'Who will ascend into heaven.'' (that is, to bring Christ down) or "Who will descend into the abyss?" (that is, to bring Christ up from the dead)."

- There is a temptation to base who you think actually made a true decision for Christ on feelings. But Scripture says that we must not do that. We should not, after we are done evangelizing, ask ourselves: "Who actually became a true disciple of Jesus Christ this day?" That is to bring Christ down from above. Also, do not ask, "Who is actually still going to hell?" That is to bring Christ up from the dead. After you are through evangelizing, simply entrust all who have made decisions, as well as those who rejected or persecuted you into Christ's hands. It is He who makes the decision of who ascends to heaven and it is He who makes the decision of who will descend into the abyss. You have done your part. You have shared the gospel. The rest is up to God and God alone!

Jason Robért

Romans 11:13 (ESV)

"...I magnify my ministry..."

- Here, Paul the Apostle speaks of magnifying (expanding) his ministry more and more (always advancing the kingdom of God). We should seek, as did the Apostle Paul, to make our ministry of evangelism bigger and bigger. You should make evangelism more and more a part of your life and you will experience more love, joy, and power in the kingdom of God. Always be seeking for ways to improve your ministry and grow it. You have a calling from Christ Jesus Himself! Be faithful to grow your ministry and the Lord will be faithful to you in ways you could have never possibly imagined!

1 Corinthians 14:32 (ESV)

"...the spirits of the prophets are subject to the prophets."

- Just as the spirits of the prophets are subject to the prophets, the spirits of the evangelists are subject to the evangelists. I strongly recommend that you seek out other evangelists who can encourage you in your ministry. They are the ones who can truly disciple you and train you to be all that you can be. They also will be compassionate with the difficulties and struggles you will face. No one can raise up an evangelist like another evangelist. Subject yourself to the evangelists and they will give you powerful insights as to how to improve and grow. I can say from over 10 years of experience that being discipled by other evangelists has greatly impacted the power and success of my ministry. No one knows how to train you to lead people to the Lord like other evangelists!

CHAPTER 7

Contact Me

- If this booklet has made an impact on you or your ministry, I would love to hear from you so that we can rejoice together!
Simply e-mail me at jrobert319@gmail.com

- Finally, if you enjoyed reading the "Salvation Stories" at the beginning of this book and the details of my ministry, you might enjoy receiving my monthly newsletter. If that is the case, just e-mail me at jrobert319@gmail.com and I would be glad to start e-mailing it to you.

CHAPTER 8

More Salvation Stories

Here are some more salvation stories, if you are interested in reading them as an encouragement to get out there and share the good news! I write these stories after each time I go out in an evangelism journal. Then, I write some of the more exciting ones as part of my monthly newsletter (which you just read about in my "Contact Me" chapter of the book).

Photographer, Maggie, Prays To Receive Christ, Brianna Confesses Christ As Her Lord and Erlinda and Destiny Get Prayed For

I went out to Seal Beach with friend, Brian. First, we went into the bakery where Miguel got saved 2 weeks ago. We found Miguel and gave him a copy of the New Testament. Joy immediately came over his face. He thanked us at least three times before we left the bakery. Then we went to the beach and passed out "God Loves You" cards to people on the beach. Finally, near the rocks, we came to a photographer named Maggie. I gave her a card and then read her John 3:16-18 and explained how God sent Jesus Christ into the world not to condemn her but to save her from her sins. She said she wanted that in her life so we joined hands and she prayed to accept Christ right there. Afterwards, we gave her a Bible and encouraged her to find a good church. Then we came to Brianna. She admitted to us that she had no assurance of her salvation. I mentioned to her that all she needs is to put Christ at the center of her life and she can have assurance. She exclaimed, "Jesus is Lord!" And we left knowing that her salvation was safe in God's hands. Finally we came to Erlinda and Destiny. Erlinda wanted us to pray for her fear of death. As I prayed, I assured her that perfect love casts out fear. I also prayed for her unsaved husband and Destiny's unsaved boyfriend. In all we talked with them for over one hour affirming to them that God is with them and has control over all the details to their lives. We left with them shouting, "Thank you! Thank you!" down the beach.

A Youth And A Homeless Man Accept Jesus Christ

I was down at Laguna Beach passing out, "Are You Going to Heaven?" gospel tracts with my Dad, Ben. We came across a young Hispanic man named Gabe who spoke perfect English. I asked him, "How would you answer that?" to the "Are You Going to Heaven?" tract. He said, "No." I said, "Would you like to know?" and he said, "Yes!" So I led him to Ephesians 2:8-9: "For it is by grace you have been saved through faith. Not by works, lest anyone should boast." And then I led him to John 3:16. Then I told him, "God died so that He could have relationship with you. Is that what you'd like?" He replied, "Yes!" And then he confessed Jesus Christ as his Lord and Savior! And he left rejoicing with me. Then someone stopped while they were reading the tract my Dad handed him. Then my Dad pointed to him for me to go talk to him about Christ. I asked him if when he died if he will go to heaven. He said, "I don't know." I asked him if he'd like to know and he said yes. Then I led him to Ephesians 2:8-9 about being saved through grace as a free gift and to John 3:16 about Christ dying for our sins. I then asked him if he'd like to make Jesus the Lord and Leader of his life. He said yes! So we prayed while I laid hands on him for the forgiveness of his sins and to make Jesus the Lord, Leader and Master of his life. It was so blessed! Then my Dad handed me a Bible to give him and I assured him of his salvation. He left filled with joy. And I was jumping for joy on the street. His name is Larry.

Youth Home Alone Comes To The Lord

I was out passing out "God Loves You" cards door to door and I came across youth named Tyler. Tyler was home alone and probably 16 years old. I showed him the card and then asked him to read the back of it out loud: "For God so loved the world that He gave His only Son that whosoever believes in him should not perish but have everlasting life. For God did not send His Son into the world to condemn the world but in order that the world might be saved through him. He who believes is not condemned. But whoever does not believe is condemned already because he has not believed in the name of the only Son of God," he read aloud. Then I explained to him that if he doesn't believe in Jesus, he's going to be punished for his sin. But that's not what God wants. It says that God sent His Son into the world to save him and mankind. "God wants to give you love, life and peace – He wants a relationship with you. Is that what you want?" I asked. "Yes!" he said. "Then pray with me!" I said. So he prayed with me to put off sin and accept Jesus Christ as his Lord, Savior and Master. I could literally feel the waves of God's love coming over him as we prayed. Gleaming, he raised his head after we were done praying. I then encouraged him to get on his bed that night and pray to Jesus! When I departed, both Tyler and me were rejoicing in what the Lord had just done.

Two Get Saved In Laguna Beach

I was giving out "Are You Going To Heaven?" tracts in Laguna Beach with a fellow evangelist named Bob and two people got saved! First, I met a man named Dominick. I asked him how he would answer the question on the tract and he said, "I don't know!" So I opened to Ephesians 2:8-9 and read him: "For it is by grace you have been saved through faith. And that is not a matter of works, lest any man should boast." I told him that grace is what saves us – it is a free gift from God that he wants to give us. He seemed very interested that salvation is a free gift. Then I read him John 3:16, "For God so loved the world that He gave His only Son that whosoever believes in Him should not perish but have everlasting life." I told him, "God wants to save you and have a relationship with you and give you love, joy and peace. Is that what you want?" "Yes!" he replied. There was so much joy in his eyes when he said yes! Then he accepted Jesus Christ as his Lord and Savior. I gave him a Bible as he was going way and he said, "Thank you! Thank you!" Then Bob started talking with a man named Chris and led him to Christ. I came up to him and gave him a list of churches he can check out in Orange County. He said, "Thank you! I live in Northern Orange County so this will help!" We also gave him a copy of the New Testament. There was so much love flooding his life it was beautiful to behold!

A Skim-Boarder In The Midst of Hecklers And A Girl Sitting In The Sand Come To The Lord

I went to Laguna Beach with my friend to give out "God Loves You" cards while walking on the beach. After passing out a few cards, we came to a group of skim boarders. I passed out cards to all of them. Two them promptly returned them saying they were Jewish. But one of the kids, named Jordan, was open. So I started sharing with him. As I was sharing, the other kids started taunting me saying, "I'm gay, am I going to hell?" I retorted, "I'm in the middle of something right now; you'll have to wait." So I kept sharing with Jordan, I read him John 3:16-18 and told him that God wants to save him from his sin and have a relationship with him filled with love, joy, peace and the presence of God. I asked, "Is that what you want?" He said yes! So we held hands in the midst of the hecklers and he accepted Jesus Christ as his Lord and Savior. After we were done praying, he jumped for joy and exclaimed, "I see the light!" Then he promptly embraced me. I then gave him a Bible together with a list of churches in Orange County he can attend. He said, "Thank you! Thank you!" Tim and I left rejoicing for his salvation and the grace He'd showed in the midst of those taunting teen-agers. It was mighty bold of Jordan to accept the Lord in the midst of his disrespectful friends. Then Tim and I came up to a girl named Cory who was sitting in the sand. I asked her if she had the love of Jesus in her life. She said, "No." So I read her John 3:16-18 and explained the good news to her.

She quickly confessed Jesus Christ as her Lord. It was so easy; she had such an open heart. Tim and I left again hugging and rejoicing at what God had done for her.

Two Youths Come to the Lord

I was going door-to-door and came to a house where there were two youths. They are friends and their names are Blake and Tyler. I gave them each a gospel card and they enthusiastically received them. Then I turned one of the cards over and read John 3:16-18 to them and explained how God doesn't want to punish them for their sins because Jesus came to die for their sins. He wants a relationship of love, joy, peace and the presence of God with them. They both said that that's what they wanted! So we prayed right there, each of them inviting Jesus Christ in to be the Lord and Savior of their lives. I was so blessed to do this with two youths. Then I gave a Bible and a list of churches to the oldest one and told him to read the book of John. That's where he can find out more about Jesus. He said he would. And I left rejoicing at their simple but profound faith!

Four Get Saved As I Was Preaching At The Orange County Rescue Mission

I was preaching on John 3:16 at the Orange County Rescue Mission. I wanted everyone there to know how much God loves them – He sent His only Son to die for their sins! I told them that if they don't believe they are already condemned and judged for their sins. But that isn't what God wants! He sent Jesus to die on the cross so that they can be saved and given love, joy peace and the Presence of God for all eternity! Many prayed to receive Christ thereafter, some 40 people. But the pastor came up and asked, "Who prayed that prayer for the first time tonight?" Four people stood up! What a joy-filled night! I left with many who wanted to shake my hand and thank me for the message. Some people embraced me. What a glorious night. I give all the glory to God for His work saving souls!

Three Saved In Laguna Beach

I was giving out "Are You Going To Heaven?" tracts in Laguna Beach with Bob and I met Dylan and Carl, two students from China. I read them Ephesians 2:8-9 and let them know that Jesus is the one who gives you the faith to believe in Him. Then I read them John 3:16 and let them know that God loves them and wants to save them. They prayed right there with me to accept Jesus Christ as their Lord and Savior and repent of their sins. I had such an inner witness of joy that they were saved - it was incredible! Praise God! Then, I met a young man named Shawn. I also led him to Ephesians 2:8-9 and told him that God wanted to give him the gift of faith so that he could believe in Jesus. The young man was smiling and seeming very interested. Then I led him to John 3:16 and told him that Jesus Christ died on the cross for his sins so that he might receive the gift of faith to believe unto eternal life. I asked him, "Is that what you want?" "Yes," he replied! So he prayed there with me to receive Jesus, repent of his sins, and receive the gift of the Holy Spirit. The boy was so excited after praying that he jumped for joy and gave me a big hug! Then we gave him a Bible, and a list of churches to attend in Orange County. What a day!

Dieter Comes To Christ

I was ministering in Laguna Beach, handing out "Are You Going To Heaven?" tracts. I met a youth named Dieter and his brother. His brother was already saved, but Dieter wasn't. So I shared Ephesians 2:8-9 with him and told him that God wanted to give him the gift of faith to believe in Jesus Christ. Then I shared John 3:16 with him and told him that God wants to save him from his sins and give him love, joy, peace and the presence of God in his life. I asked him if that what he wanted and he said, "Yes!" So we prayed for him to repent of his sins and declared that Jesus Christ died for his sins and that God would give him the gift of the Holy Spirit. When he left I could literally feel the presence of God and so I rejoiced that another soul just entered the book of life!

Two Saved In Seal Beach

I went with my friend Brian Aschbrenner to Seal Beach to pass out "God Loves You" cards. We walked into a bakery and bought cookies from a man named Jesse. I gave him a card and read him John 3:16-18 on the back of the card. I told him that God wants to save him from hell and condemnation and give him life, love, joy, peace and the Presence of God instead. I asked him if that's what he wants and he said, "Yes!" then he made a confession of faith and I gave him a Bible and list of 46 churches in Orange County with their web addresses to check out. Brian and I left rejoicing in God's saving grace. Then we went to the beach and passed out more cards. Then Brian met a girl named Andrea. He gave her a card and read her John 3:16-18. She said she believed and accepted Christ right there. I could feel the awesome presence of the Holy Spirit over all we did this day. I thank God for His awesome pleasure in what we are doing. It was literally the first person to get saved through someone who I have been discipling to share the gospel! So, for that, I praise God!

Samantha Comes To Faith In Laguna Beach

I was in Laguna Beach passing out "Are You Going To Heaven?" gospel tracts and I met a teenager named Samantha. She said she didn't know what would happen after she dies. So I led her to Ephesians 2:8-9 and told her that God wants to give her the gift of faith to believe in Jesus Christ. She was very animated and excited about that! Then I led her to John 3:16 and told her of God's love and desire to save her from hell and give her eternal life instead. I asked her if she wanted that and she said yes! So we held hands and prayed that Jesus would come and be the Lord and Savior of her life. She repented of her sins and accepted the gift of the Holy Spirit! It was a blessed experience and she was very happy with her decision. We parted rejoicing at what God had done for her!

Door-To-Door Ministry Yields A Harvest

I was going door-to-door and came across two youths on their front lawn named Dominic and Rocco. I gave them both "God Loves You" cards. I asked if I could read them the back of the card (John 3:16-18). They said that would be okay. So I read it to them and explained to them that because of our sin, God sent His only Son into the world to a live a sinless life and be sacrificed for our sins. Right then, Rocco said, "I believe!" I asked Dominic if he believe too and he said he did! So I asked them to pray with me right there on their lawn. They repented of their sins, confessed Jesus Christ as their Lord and Savior, and asked for the gift of the Holy Spirit. By this time, the presence of God's love was so strong I could feel it rushing into them! We all left rejoicing and praising God for what He had done!

Five Come To The Lord At Seal Beach

I was going evangelizing at Seal Beach with my friend, Brian. We were giving out "God Loves You" cards and five people made decisions for Christ! First, we came up to three girls, one of whom knew the Lord and two did not. The ones who did not were named Jenny and Leslie. I quickly gave them a "God Loves You" cards and read to them John 3:16-18. I told them that God wants to have a relationship with them in the Holy Spirit. Immediately, Jenny and Leslie's faces brightened and said that they would like that! So I prayed with them to put off their sins and put on the Holy Spirit. They confessed Jesus Christ as Lord of their lives and the Holy Spirit entered them. We talked with them longer and then left rejoicing and hugging because of what Jesus had done for them. Then, we came to a man playing rap music on his stereo. We gave him a card and told him that Jesus loves him. We asked him if he had a relationship with Jesus Christ and he said, "No." Then I read him John 3:16-18 and told him that he was already condemned, but that's not what God wants. God came to save him and give him eternal life. Then he said that he wanted that, that he'd been in prison and people had told him of John 3:16 but he's never done anything with it. Then I prayed with him to accept Jesus Christ as his Lord and Savior and to put off all former sins. It was a joyous experience! His name is Steven. Then, we came to a man named Jesus (Hispanic). His wife was saved but he was not. Brian shared the gospel with him and his wife was overwhelmed with joy at what we were saying to him. Then he accepted the Lord as his Savior. It was so joyful to see someone I trained lead someone to Christ! Finally, we came to a man named Pedro. He was hardened and walking on the fence of faith. He said, "I don't want to accept Jesus today." But I told him, "Today is the day of salvation!" Finally, after much talking back and forth, the man admitted his need for Christ and prayed with me to accept Jesus as his Lord and personal Savior. Brian and I left the beach giving each other high-fives and hugging as we rejoiced in God's work that beautiful day!

Baptism In Laguna Beach

I went to Laguna Beach to baptize a friend of mine named Evelyn. Her husband stood on the shore taking pictures as we made our way through the waves. I asked her two questions before I baptized her: "Have you repented of all your known sin?" and, "Who is the only Lord and Savior of your life?" Her answers were: "Yes" and "Jesus"! So I baptized her in the name of the Father, the Son and the Holy Spirit. She came out of the water rejoicing with me! Afterwards, when we were out for coffee, she said she felt like a void had been filled in her life. Praise God! Amen!

Baptism At Pirate's Cove

I went to Big Corona to Pirate's Cove to baptize Rico. Rico had brought his Tarot Cards (Satanic cards used in predicting one's future) and we buried them in the sand to be rid of them once and for all! It was a big deal to Rico to finally get rid of them somewhere no one else can ever use them. We went into the water and I asked Rico who his Lord and Savior is. "Jesus," was his reply. Then I asked him if he ever wanted to sin again. "No," was his reply. So, then I baptized him there in the name of Jesus Christ, in the name of the Father, the Son and the Holy Spirit. As he was coming up from the water, I sensed the power of God coming upon him to do His goodwill and pleasure. We gave each other high-fives and went back to the shore rejoicing in what had just transpired. It was a blessed day. Rico had accepted the Lord and been baptized in only two days. God is powerfully at work in his life! Amen.

A Great, New Evangelistic Soil

I just found a great, new evangelistic soil! High school campuses! I could literally feel the power of God's anointing of love pulsing through me! Angel and Brianna both accepted Jesus Christ as their Lord and Savior through the "Are You Going To Heaven?" gospel tract. An elder woman tried to stop me evangelizing by shouting out her window: "You need to get away from these kids or I'm going to call the police!" But I was on a public street and legal so I just ignored the empty threat. Satan was trying to stop the youth from getting saved! And God wouldn't let him. I gave Brianna a Bible and she's going to start reading the book of John. Praise Jesus!

Three Come To The Lord At El Toro High School

Three young men just got saved!!! I was passing out "Are You Going To Heaven?" gospel tracts outside of El Toro High School and I met Anthony, a football player. I shared the whole gospel with him and he said he wanted to get saved, but just not today. So I said, "You know, it says, 'Today is the day of salvation.' You know about today but you and I don't know if we have a tomorrow!" He was convicted and then said, "Yes, I'd like salvation." So he prayed with me on the corner to accept Jesus Christ, put off his sins and accept the Holy Spirit. It was a blessed encounter! Then, I met Kevin who was kind of depressed. But when I shared the love of Jesus Christ with him, he brightened up. He then confessed Jesus Christ as his Lord and accepted a Bible and list of churches he can attend. I pointed him to the book of John and he said he'd read it. Praise God! Then I met Carlos. He admitted to me that he doesn't know what would happen if he died. So I pointed him to Ephesians 2:8-9 and John 3:16. He began to get really excited! He wanted so badly to have hope in the next life. So we grabbed hands and he prayed to accept Jesus Christ as his Lord and Savior. High school campuses are ripe for the harvest! Amen!

Five El Toro High School Students Come To The Lord

Five El Toro High School students just accepted Jesus Christ as their Lord and Savior! The harvest is truly plentiful! All I did was read then Ephesians 2:8-9 and tell them that God wants to give them the gift of faith to believe that Jesus Christ died on the cross for their sins and then lead them to John 3:16. I told them that Jesus died for their sins and wants to give them eternal life instead of hell and condemnation. Then Shane, Andrew, Brenda, Lisa, and Alma each prayed individually to invite Jesus Christ into hearts to be their Lord and Savior. They repented of their sins and received the Holy Spirit of promise! It was such an amazing harvest! Each and every student who wasn't already a Christian accepted Jesus Christ as Lord and Savior today. I left rejoicing in the Holy Ghost!

Five More El Toro Students Receive Christ

I went again to El Toro High School, passing out "Are You Going To Heaven?" tracts. Today another five people made decisions for Christ! I shared Ephesians 2:8-9 and John 3:16 with them and Michael, Jason, Luca, Addie and Josh all accepted Jesus Christ as their Lord and Savior! Jason believed that if he was just good enough he'd go to heaven. But I explained to him that you can only enter by faith in Jesus Christ. Then I shared that God loves him and wants to give him eternal life and then he said he wanted that! So he prayed with me to receive salvation. Then there was Luca who was an agnostic. He told me, "Honestly, I don't think that much about it [God/Heaven/Hell]." But after I shared that God loves him and wants to give him the gift of eternal life, he was so excited, he received Christ right there! Then there was Addie. She hadn't really thought much about Heaven and Hell. But she received the words of Christ with much joy! She accepted Christ, prayed with me and received a Bible and promised to read the book of John. Then, there was Josh who was apprehensive. But, upon hearing the word of faith, he immediately accepted it and prayed with me to accept Jesus as his Lord and Savior, put off his sins and receive the gift of the Holy Spirit. It was such a blessed day and I left blessing God for all He had done!

Harvest At El Toro High School

I was just evangelizing at El Toro High School and five high school students just gave their lives to the Lord! Their names are: Kevin, Cameron, Saul, Prestley, and Brandon. Kevin was resistant when I first met him; he said, "I'm not religious!" but after sharing with Him that God wants to give him the faith to believe and that Jesus died on the cross for his sins, he quickly said he wanted eternal life. He prayed with me right there to receive his salvation. Then I met Cameron who was walking with a resistant friend. But I kept preaching the word in spite of it; I sensed God moving on Cameron's life. When I asked whether either of them wanted to receive salvation, Cameron said, "I would!" So we prayed that he would enter the kingdom of God and that God would forgive his sins. Then I met Saul, a Hispanic young man. He said he didn't know where he'd go after he dies. So I shared with him that God wants to give him the faith to believe that Jesus died on the cross for his sins. He eyes lit up! Then I shared that God loves him and wants to give him eternal life. I asked, "Do you want that?" He said, "Yes!" so we immediately prayed that he would renounce his sins and receive salvation in Jesus Christ our Lord. Then, I met a young woman named Prestley. She was listening to music and walking when I came up to her. But she took off her head phones and began to listen. She was so receptive! She gave her life to Jesus Christ immediately after hearing the good news. Finally, I met Brandon. He was young – probably in 9th grade. But I shared that Jesus died for his sins and wants to give him the faith to believe that. He then said he wanted Christ as his Lord and Savior. So we prayed there on the street and he entered into the book of life. I left rejoicing at how plentiful the harvest is at El Toro High School. Praise be to Almighty God!

Two Young Men Get Saved At Seal Beach

I was evangelizing in Seal Beach with my friend, Brian, and two young men got saved! Spencer and Joey were both riding their skateboards and I stopped them to give them a "God Loves You" card. They were both friends when I read them John 3:16-18. I let them know that if they didn't believe in Jesus they were already condemned. But that isn't what God wants for their lives. God did not send His Son into the world to condemn them but to save them and give them eternal life – love, joy, peace and the presence of the Holy Spirit. I asked them, "Is that what you want?" and they both said, "Yes!" Joey is Jewish so he said, "Yes... this is all new to me." So I asked them to pray with me to receive eternal life. And they did! Some of Joey's friends were making fun of him when he prayed so we just ignored them and continued to pray. They each renounced their sins, accepted Jesus Christ as their Lord and Savior and asked for the gift of the Holy Spirit. It was a blessed day to say the least!

Six Give Their Lives To The Lord At El Toro High School

Today I ministered at El Toro High School and six youths got saved! Their names are Caesar, Sharleen, Nicholas, Angel,

Omar and Saul. Caesar is Hispanic. I had already passed out a tract to his friend on a prior day, but today it was Caesar's time! I shared with him that God wanted to give him the faith to believe. He was initially apprehensive, but after I went over the prayer of salvation on the back of the form and explained what God wants of him, God powerfully moved and he gave his life to Christ. He prayed to repent of his sins and accepted Jesus Christ as the Lord and Savior of his life. There was so much joy within me at his salvation! Then, I met Sharleen. She too was apprehensive. But after I told her of God's love for her and how He died to give her eternal life, she gladly accepted His invitation by praying to renounce her sins and inviting Jesus Christ to be the Lord and Savior of her life. I gave her a Bible, as I give to everyone who comes to faith, and showed her the book of John to read, my contact information, a list of 46 churches she can attend. She gladly accepted the gift and left thanking me! Then, I met Nicholas. He was very receptive and asked what he needed to do to be saved. So I showed him the prayer to pray and we prayed through it – to accept Jesus Christ as the Lord and Savior of his life. When I was driving home and saw some young students walking on the side of the street. The Spirit inspired me to stop my car and share with them. They were very receptive! Angel, Omar and Saul all accepted Jesus and prayed to renounce their sins and receive Jesus Christ as the Lord and Savior of their lives. There was so much excitement on Saul's face as he read through the tract! He wanted salvation and Jesus was already loving on him when I asked him to pray to receive Jesus as Lord and Savior as the others had done. I left rejoicing at how God had brought six students into his everlasting kingdom today! It was a miracle!

Seven El Toro High School Students Come To The Lord

I just went evangelizing again at El Toro High School and seven students made decisions for Christ! Their names are Juan, Elias, Jeremy, Christian, Jessica, Ethan and Miguel. Time would fail if I wrote down all of their stories, but here are a few. I met Jeremy who was an enthusiastic young man. I told him of God's love for him and how Jesus Christ died for his sins. He smiled and became even more enthusiastic! He said, "Yes," when I asked, "Would you like eternal life?" Then, he prayed with me on the sidewalk to receive Jesus Christ as his Lord and Savior. Then I came to Jessica. Jessica was in a rush to get to her mom's car. So I merely read her John 3:16. Immediately, the Holy Spirit rushed all over her and her disposition turned to joy. She said she wanted eternal life and relationship with God! So she and I prayed together for her to enter eternal life and put off her sins. It was a joy-filled, blessed experience. Then, I met Miguel together with a whole group of cyclists. He was walking and I stopped to ask him, "Are You Going To Heaven?" He said, "I don't know." So I told him that according to Ephesians 2:8-9, faith is a gift from God to receive to believe in Jesus Christ's death and resurrection. He began smiling and looking intently at the tract. Then, I shared God's love with him and he gave his life to Christ right there by praying with me to put off his sins, believe in Jesus and enter everlasting life. It was such a blessed day!

Two More El Toro Students Receive Christ

I was standing on the corner at El Toro High School and I met Brenda and Clair. I asked them "Are You Going To

Heaven?" and they responded, "I don't know." So I led them to Ephesians 2:8-9 and told them that God wants to give them the faith to believe that Jesus died for their sins. Then I opened to John 3:16 and told them about God's love and offer of eternal life. He wants to given them love, joy, peace and the presence of the Holy Spirit. They the both said, "Yes!" when I asked them if that's what they want. Then, they prayed with me to accept Jesus Christ as their Lord and Savior. I gave them each a Bible and a list of 46 churches in Orange County they can attend. I left them filled with joy – they had been smiling with they made their decisions for Christ.

Harvesting At Seal Beach

I went out evangelizing at Seal Beach with my friend, Brian, and four people made decisions for Christ! Their names are Marc, Jose, Alexis and Rene. First, we met Marc and Jose. They were sitting outside an ice cream shop on the street. I asked if I could give them a "God Loves You" card and they said, "Yes." Then I told them of God's love for them and that all those who don't believe in Jesus are already condemned, but that isn't what God wants. He sent His only Son to die on the cross for their sins so that they could have eternal life. I asked them if that's what they wanted and they said, "Yes!" So I lead them in a prayer, they renounced their sins and made Jesus Christ the Lord and Savior of their lives. Their faces were gleaming with smiles as they prayed. It was so blessed; I could literally feel God smiling at us as we lead them to a decision for Christ. Then I met Alexis. She was reading a sign by the Pier and I gave her a card. I ready the back of the card to her (John 3:16-18) and she said that she'd like a relationship with Jesus Christ.

So we prayed right there for Christ to enter her life. I was so excited. Finally, we met Rene. He was fishing on the pier with his dad and sister. I asked if I could read him the back of the card and he said, "Yes." Then, I told him that God wants an eternal relationship with him filled with love, joy, peace and the Holy Spirit. He said he wanted that so we prayed right there and he invited Jesus Christ in to be the Lord and Savior of his life. He was so happy. We gave him a Bible and told him to read the book of John to learn more about Jesus who he'd just accepted. It was a divine appointment. And Brian and I gave each other high-fives as we were walking and left the beach. What a day!

In One Day, 16 Give Their Lives To The Lord At Trabuco Hills High School

It was truly a blessed day! I went to Trabuco Hills High School for the first time to share the gospel. 16 students made decisions for Christ! Their names are Brian, Jake, Chloe, Scylla, Angelo, Brendan, Rachael, Dion, Brian, Fredrick, Amaranta, David, Brian, Oscar, Eric and Aido. It was the most fruitful day in my entire ministry! Everyone I talked with made decisions for Christ. I simply passed out the "Are You Going To Heaven?" tract and let the people know that God wants to give them the faith to believe that Jesus died and rose again for their sins and that God loves them and wants to give them eternal life, which is love, joy, peace and the presence of the Holy Spirit. I met Angelo, smoking next to his home. He had tattoos all over. I handed him a tract and preached the gospel to him and he said, "Yeah, I'd actually like that [Jesus]!" So we prayed right there and he put off his sins and accepted Jesus Christ as Lord and Savior. Chloe and Scylla were riding their bikes home so I stopped them and preached the good news to them. They were so quick to respond – they said, "Yes, we'd like that!" So they prayed aloud with me to accept Jesus Christ as their Lord and Savior. The biggest harvest came when I preached to three guys walking home from school named David, Brian and Oscar. They all received the good news with smiles on their faces and prayed to enter the kingdom of God. There were so many others who made decisions with joy on their faces this day. I passed out all of my Bibles and gave out all of my lists of churches to attend. It was a glorious, joy-filled day!

Two Trabuco Hills High School Students Come To The Lord

I just went to Trabuco Hills High School and passed out "Are You Going To Heaven?" tracts. A girl named Shauna and a guy named Charlie both made decisions for Christ! I talked with Shauna and shared God's love for her and his desire to show her love, joy, peace and the presence of the Holy Spirit. I asked her if she wanted that and she made a declaration of faith with joy. It was a blessed encounter! Then, I met Charlie. He already had a Bible and had been reading it but had never made Jesus Christ the Lord and Savior of his life. I asked him if he'd like to and he prayed, "God, please save me!" and he made Jesus his Lord and Savior. Then we waved to each other as he drove off in his car. God truly touched him. Also, a student from a previous day called to me: "Hey, Jason!" and we waved at and greeted each other as he went into school. I love it when God confirms your work when students remember you and give thanks at the work you've done in their lives!

A Laguna Beach Harvest

I went to Laguna Beach and was handing out "Are You Going To Heaven?" tracts together with my Dad. We met Gary and Dakota. I shared with them that God wants to give them the gift of faith to believe that Jesus died for their sins. Then I shared God's love for them and His desire to save them. I asked them, "Is that what you want?" They both said, "Yes!" And I then led them in a prayer of salvation. Then my Dad got out two Bibles and lists of churches to give to them. They were so excited to receive them! You could see the gratitude and excitement in their eyes! They said, "Thank you! Thank you!" And I told them to read the book of John. They hinted they would. And then shook my hand and departed with joy on their faces. It was a blessed encounter between them and the Living God! And Jesus Christ added two more into His glorious kingdom!

Seven Make Decisions For Christ At Trabuco Hills High School

I was just at Trabuco Hill High School passing out "Are You Going To Heaven?" tracts and seven students made decisions for Christ. Their names are Lauren, Alex, Anthony, Jay, Omar, Torrey, and Abraham. It was such a joy-filled day! When I met Jay and explained the gospel to him, he said, "Honestly, that's something I want." So he prayed to renounce his sins and make Jesus Christ the Lord and Savior of his life. Then, I met Omar. He was walking with a Christian, but was unsaved himself. So he listened as I preached the good news to him. Then he said he wanted Jesus Christ as his Lord and Savior. So we prayed together. As we prayed, Omar's face lit up with joy! After I gave him a Bible and list of churches to attend, he thanked me and thanked me! Then he shook my hand. I could tell, the Holy Spirit truly moved on his life. It was a God-encounter for him. Then, I met Torrey and Abraham who were boyfriend and girlfriend. I preached the good news of God's free gift of eternal life to them and both said they wanted to be saved. Torrey couldn't stop smiling as we prayed to invite Jesus Christ in to be the Lord and Savior of their lives. I thank God for the abundant harvest he is working at Trabuco Hills High School! Praise God!

Two Get Saved At Trabuco Hills High School

Today I went to Trabuco Hills High School and passed out "Are You Going To Heaven?" tracts. A girl named Sienna and a guy named Marcus both made decisions for Christ. I shared the good news of God's love with them and the free gift of eternal life and they both accepted Jesus Christ as their Lord and Savior. As they were praying to receive Jesus Christ into their lives, Sienna prayed so boldly it really shocked me! She so wanted to enter into God's Kingdom – she was passionate about it! We left shaking hands and rejoicing in God's saving work on the cross.

Jose Gives His Life To The Lord At Laguna Beach

I was at the beach evangelizing with three other evangelists who normally come with me to Laguna Beach on Saturdays. I gave an "Are You Going To Heaven?" gospel tract to a young man named Jose. I read him Ephesians 2:8-9 and told him that God wants to give him the gift of faith to believe that Jesus Christ died for his sins. Then, I shared John 3:16 with him and told him that God loves him and wants to give him eternal life. I asked him if that what he wanted and he said, "Yes!" so we prayed together that God would forgive his sins and make Jesus Christ the Lord and Savior of his life! It was such a blessed occasion. I could literally feel the Holy Spirit of eternal life within me going into him. His mom was standing by smiling and affirming what just happened. I love it when the parents of those who are led to Christ rejoice with me. I gave him a copy of the New Testament and told him to read the book of John. It was such a joy to get to participate in the saving work of God this day!

Nine Students Come To Christ At Trabuco Hills High School

I went to Trabuco Hills High School to pass out "Are You Going To Heaven?" gospel tracts and nine students gave their lives to the Lord Jesus Christ! Their names are Riley, Braden, Ivan, Brandon, James, Jesus, Crystal, Kevin and Brandon. I used the same approach with them all. I shared Ephesians 2:8-9 with them and told them how God wants to give them the gift of faith to believe in Jesus Christ death on the cross for their sins. Then, I read them John 3:16 and told them about God's love and His free gift of eternal life. I told them that God wants them to abide in love, joy, peace and the presence of the Holy Spirit. And they all said they wanted that! The young man, Jesus, was initially hostile to the gospel, however. He said plainly, "I am going to hell!" But after I read those verses to him and explained God's love to Him, his heart melted and he said, "Yes. I want that!" then he prayed to accept Jesus Christ as Lord and Savior. Afterwards, he was so excited he wanted to shake my hand and thank me for the Bible he'd received. I could literally see the joy in his eyes! Praise God for setting apart these nine students. I pray that they go to one of the churches I connected them with. Amen!

Eight Make Decisions For Christ At Trabuco Hills High School

I went evangelizing at Trabuco Hills High School and eight students made decisions for Christ! Their names were Lisa, Kyle, Osmar, Bryce, Gideon, Tyler, Willey, and Royce. As I was talking with two guys, one said that he was a Christian and one said that he didn't believe in Heaven. So I focused on the later. I told him that Jesus Christ died on the cross to give him the gift of faith that He died for his sins. I then told him that God loves him and wants to give him eternal life – love, joy, peace and the presence of the Holy Spirit. Then he had a change of heart and believed my message! We then prayed for him to enter the Kingdom of God. He repented of his sins and asked for the gift of the Holy Spirit. His name was Bryce. It was such a joy to see his faith turn from the things of this world to eternal, spiritual things. I gave him a Bible and he thanked me and said he'd read the book of John. It was a truly blessed experience! Then, many other students made similar decisions for Christ! I rejoiced and called and texted my prayer team to let them know about the abundant harvest so that they could share the joy with me. It was a truly blessed day! Praise the Living God!

Five Get Saved At Trabuco Hills High School

I was at Trabuco Hills High School sharing the gospel with my friend Nick and five students gave their lives to the Lord Jesus!

Their names are Adam, Kyle, Nick, Henry and Kevin. When we met Nick, he was standing there with an uninterested friend. But Nick was interested. I shared with him Ephesians 2:8-9 and told him that God wants to give him the gift of faith to believe that Jesus Christ died and rose for his sins. Then I shared with him John 3:16 and told him that God loves him and wants to save him from hell and give him eternal life. Immediately he accepted the message and prayed with me to put off his sins and accept Jesus Christ as his Lord and Savior! He was so excited when he received a Bible from us as a gift. He said, "I've been wanting a Bible!" He was already seeking spiritual things but this day was the day of his actualization in Christ! He shook my hand and Nick's hand and thanked us. Praise God for His harvesting work!

Johon Turns To Christ At Trabuco Hills High School

I went evangelizing at Trabuco Hills High School and 14 students gave their lives to the Lord. Their names are Bertine, Ann, William, Andrew, Noah, Spencer, Francisco, Jeffery, Huber, Johon, Jeosaphon, Jake, Jenny and Eric. When I came to Huber, Johon and Jeosaphon, I had some resistance. Johon would simply not believe that there was a hell. But when I shared Ephesians 2:8-9 and John 3:16, it melted his heart and he insisted on coming to Christ and so did his friends Huber and Jeosaphon. They prayed with me to put off their sins and accepted Jesus Christ as their personal Lord and Savior. It was a blessed encounter! The rest of the students that came to the Lord came this day came so easily! It was like Jesus Christ was there with me calling them to Himself! What a harvest we had! 14 students in just one day! Praise Jesus and God the Father!

Three Come To The Lord At Seal Beach

I was in Seal Beach with my friend Brian Aschbrenner and three people made decisions for Christ. There names were Mitchell, Shay and Nathan. Mitchell and Shay were friends and we passed out a "God Loves You" card to them. We told them that, if they don't believe in Jesus Christ as their Lord and Savior, then they are already condemned. But that's not what God wants! He sent His only Son into the world, not to condemn it, but to save it. I asked them if they both want to make Jesus the Lord of their lives and they both said, "Yes!" So we prayed that they would put off their sins and they accepted the Holy Spirit of Jesus Christ into their hearts forever! I then gave them both Bibles and a list of Churches to check out in their own neighborhoods. We parted rejoicing with them; praising God for what He had done in their lives! Then, Brian and I were sharing the gospel with two men. They said they wanted to accept Christ, but at home privately. Then, one of their sons exclaimed boldly (who had been listening to the whole thing), "I want Jesus Christ!" So we prayed for him to enter the Kingdom of God by renouncing his sins and accepting Jesus Christ as his Lord and Savior. I thank God for the childlike faith of this youth. He will be blessed forever because of his decision!

Joseph And Emanuel's Decision

I was at Trabuco Hills High School on a minimum day – so there were only three students I talked with. Two of them accepted Jesus Christ as their Lord and Savior! I went over Ephesians 2:8-9 and John 3:16 with them and they quickly said they wanted eternal life in Jesus Christ our Lord. So I prayed with them to enter the Kingdom of God. They left shaking my hand and thanking me. I thank God for Joseph and Emanuel's decision to accept the Lord Jesus Christ!!!

Tomas Departs With Joy

I just went to Trabuco Hills High School and passed out "Are You Going To Heaven?" tracts. Three people gave their lives to the Lord. Their names are Eric, Bertine and Thomas. When I came to Thomas, he said he wasn't sure about whether or not he was going to heaven. So I read him Ephesians 2:8-9 and told him that God wants to give him the faith to believe that Jesus Christ died for his sins. Then, I shared John 3:16 and told him of God's love for him and His plan to give him eternal life. When I finished preaching the gospel to him, I asked him, "Would you like that [eternal life]?" He emphatically said, "I'd love that!" so we prayed to renounce his sins and accept Jesus Christ as his Lord and Savior. He left shaking my hand with his own new Bible and rejoicing! You should have seen his smile and the joy on his face after he made that decision! Bless God! Praise His Holy name!

10 Come To Christ In Laguna Beach

School was out so I decided to go to Laguna Beach to share the good news using my "Are You Going To Heaven?" tract. Ten people made decisions for Christ! Their names are Caesar, Christopher, Matt, Dylan, Will, Brian, Boe, Morgan, Brian and Jackie. When I came to Caesar and Christopher, I came to a whole Hispanic family. The Mom was a Christian but the Dad and the children were not. So I shared the good news with Caesar and Christopher. I told them that God is just looking for them to put their faith in Jesus Christ and that God loves them and wants to give them eternal life. Both of them readily accepted the gospel and Jesus Christ and prayed with me for a relationship with Jesus Christ. They were so excited to receive their Bibles and Christopher said that he wants to read the Book of John. It was especially blessed because his mother is already a Christian and looking for a church. I told her about my Church (Compass Bible Church) and she said she wanted to attend. So she looked it up on her iPhone and said she'd go there. I thank God for His movement on this family. Then I came to Boe and Morgan who are boyfriend and girlfriend. They were just enjoying a sunny day on the beach when I came to them. They both said they wanted Christ in their lives, so we prayed that Jesus would enter their hearts. Morgan broke down crying in the middle of the prayer! She was so overwhelmed that both her and Boe received Christ together on this great day! It was a blessed encounter. I gave them each Bibles and a list of churches to attend. They were so grateful. When I walked back their way a half and hour later they were each holding their tract and Bible tightly to their chests. I think they were reading the Bible together. We smiled and waved to each other as we rejoiced at God's good work in them. I felt the Holy Spirit impress on me the verse in 1 John: "If you keep my Word (Logos), truly the love of God is perfected in you." That's exactly the way I felt, as I had loved on so many people that day. It was too overwhelming to take in. I can't believe that God has used me in His ministry of love to the lost. It is such an amazing blessing and honor! Praise the Lord Jesus Christ!

Young Man Is Stoked To Be Reading The Bible I Gave Him The Day Before

I went evangelizing again to Trabuco Hills High School, passing out "Are You Going To Heaven?" gospel tract and two young men came to Christ. Their names are Armando and Daniel. When I met Armando, I immediately dropped all of my gospel tracts all over the street. And, as I was picking them up, Armando waited patiently by. The Holy Spirit was at work. Then I told him that the Holy Spirit wants to give him the gift of faith to believe that Jesus Christ died for his sins. His eyes lit up! "That's what I want!" he said. So we prayed right there for him to enter the Kingdom of God and make Jesus Christ his Lord and Savior! Right after we got done talking, a young man with blue braces came up to me, "I'm reading the Book of John just like you told me too!" he declared. He had received Christ the day before and was so excited to be reading his Bible! I told him, "In the beginning the Word was with God and the Word was God. And the Word became flesh and dwelt among us and we beheld His glory, the glory of the only Son of the Father." He loved that! "God became Jesus Christ and manifested Himself to the world to let the world know who He is. It's all in the Bible! Keep reading the Book of John and you'll see!" I told him. The young man was so excited about the Word of God! He had been telling his friends about it. He said he'd keep reading the Word. It was another blessed encounter and I was blessed to know my work is bearing fruit! Praise God Almighty!

A Blessed Day At Seal Beach

I went evangelizing at Seal Beach with my friend, Brian, passing out "God Loves You" cards. By God's grace, we led five people to decisions for Christ. Their names are Zac, Pedro, Eddie, Juan and Alex. First, Brian noticed a sad looking young man named Zac. Brian went to talk to him and handed him a "God Loves You" card. Immediately, Zac said, "This is exactly what I need!" Then, Brian explained to him that the wages of sin is death, but the free gift of God is eternal life in Jesus Christ our Lord. The young man said that he wanted eternal life so Brian urged him to pray with him. So they prayed that Zac put off his sins and accept Jesus Christ as his personal Lord and Savior. Then, they prayed that God give Zac the promised Holy Spirit. It made me so proud to see Brian flourishing and leading someone to the Lord! It was a God-ordained encounter. Next, I met five Hispanic men about to head to the beach. I passed out my card to four of them and then preached the gospel to them. I told them that if they don't believe, they are already condemned, but that's not what God wants. He sent his only Son to give them eternal life, which is relationship with Him, the one true God and Jesus Christ whom He sent. Then I asked them if that's what they want. Three of them said they did! So they prayed with me to put off their sins and trust in Jesus Christ as their personal Lord and Savior. They were so excited to receive the Bibles we gave them afterward. They wanted to read the book of John and check into the churches from the church list we gave them. It was such a blessed day preaching the Good News at Seal Beach!

14 Students Give Their Lives To The LORD In One Day

I went to Mission Viejo High School, passed out the "Are You Going To Heaven?" tract and 14 students gave their lives to

Christ. Their names are Alex, Chris, Ian, Amelio, Ian, Conner, Aidan, Destiny, Jenny, Aida, Gabe, Tiffany, Jessica and Ethan. When I came to Destiny, Jenny, and Aida, God gave me great boldness declaring the good news of eternal life in Jesus Christ to them. Their hearts were immediately turned to serve the living God. I asked them to pray with me to accept Christ and they did so with laughter. I felt the pressure of the students around them made them nervous; that's why they prayed with nervous laughter. But that didn't stop them! They renounced all their sins and made Jesus Christ the Lord and Savior of their lives! I gave them each a Bible and a list of nearby churches to attend. They said they would read the book of John. I praise God for allowing me to see their faith, faith that He gave them. We departed praising the Lord. The rest of the students who came to Christ this day did so in such humility, it startled me. It was as though God was making His appeal to them through me. And for this honor, I can only bless and thank my Lord and God, Jesus Christ!

Nine Students Come To Christ At Mission Viejo High School

I went out to evangelize at Mission Viejo High School using the "Are You Going To Heaven?" gospel tract. Nine students gave their lives to Christ! Their names are Christian, Vanessa, Chris, Joaquin, Chris, Emily, Paula, Spencer and Tyler. When I came to Chris and Emily, God granted me great favor with them. I preached the good news to them using my tract and they both said they wanted to give their lives to Christ. So I led them in a prayer of salvation. What surprised me was how incredibly bold their prayer was. They each proclaimed to the Lord: "Lord Jesus, I believe that You died on the cross for my sins. I repent of my sins. Thank you for forgiving me my sins. Please give me eternal life and the precious gift of the Holy Spirit! In Your name I pray. Amen!" And, so they both entered the Kingdom of God! They thanked me for coming to them and accepted the Bible and list of local churches they can go to. I praise God that they were so zealous to enter His Kingdom and that God used me for His great work!!! Praise be to the LORD!

Another Eight Students Come To The LORD At Mission Viejo High School

I went out to Mission Viejo High School and used the "Are You Going To Heaven?" gospel tract to lead students to our blessed Savior. God gave me such grace among the students that eight of them accepted Jesus Christ as their personal Lord and Savior! Their names are James, John, Ramon, Chris, Thomas, James, Justin, and Elia. When I came to Justin and Elia, they were both sitting on a bench outside of the nearby Starbucks on La Paz Rd. I presented with them the good news that God wants to give them the faith to believe in Jesus Christ for everlasting life, which is that they may know Him the only True God and Jesus Christ whom He sent. They both said that they wanted to have this blessed relationship. I felt the Lord powerfully move among them just as they made that decision. And they both prayed with me to enter eternal life! Justin was holding the gospel tract in his hands like someone would gently hold a newborn baby and, when I gave them each Bibles, he grasped the Bible to his chest in love for God! I told them to start out by reading the gospel of John and both said that they would. It

Jason Robért

was such a blessed encounter. I parted ways with them blessing God for bringing them into the kingdom of Jesus Christ!

24 Come To Christ In Seal Beach In One Afternoon

I went to Seal Beach to share the gospel with my friend Brian Aschbrenner, and we had the best day so far in my evangelistic career – 24 people gave their lives to Christ Jesus. Their names are Eric, Mario, Fabian, Devin, Edith, Isaac, Jesus, Patti, Sandra, Allison, LaShanay, Brianna, A family of seven (I can't remember all of their names), Kimberly, Carina, George, Steven, and Ashley. We first came to a group of high school boys. And I preached the good news to all of them. Then, they all scattered and one was left standing there named Fabian. He asked desperately, "Do I have to be perfect to be a Christian?" So I answered, "No! You only need to try to be righteous before God. And, when you do sin, confess your sins to God so that he can forgive you." The he said with glee, "So I don't have to be perfect!" I answered, "No. Just try your best to do God's will. And then repent whenever you do sin." This pleased Fabian very much. Then, Brian and I lead him in prayer to renounce his sins and trust in Jesus Christ for salvation and everlasting life. We gave him a Bible to read and a list of churches in Orange County and the surrounding cities to attend. He said he'd read the Bible! Bless God! We parted with him with high-fives and praising the Lord of our salvation! Later, after many more were saved, we ran out of "God Loves You" cards and so began passing out "Are You Going To Heaven?" gospel tracts. Eventually, we came upon a family of seven and asked them if they were going to heaven. None of them answered, "Yes," so I preached the good news of Jesus' death on the cross for our

- 98 -

eternal life. Then, every one of them, from the parents to the children, said that they wanted to be saved! So I led them in a group prayer to renounce their sins and trust in Jesus Christ for eternal salvation! It was incredible! I've never led that many people to the Lord at once before. It was as if the Holy Spirit was passing through Brian and I in a stream of Living Water to all the thirsty on the entire beach! We left this family rejoicing in the Holy Spirit. I can't remember a time when I've felt the presence of God so powerfully among us. I can't believe that 24 people entered life through the Holy Spirit of Jesus Christ's work through us in one afternoon! All glory be to God Most High!

Nine Students Give Their Lives To The Lord Jesus

I went to Mission Viejo High School to pass out the "Are You going To Heaven?" gospel tract and nine students gave their lives to Christ Jesus! Their names are Alex, Josh, Alfredo, Dallas, Anthony, Min-Fay, Kyler, Katie, and Matt. When I came to Anthony, he was especially open to hearing the gospel. I preached the good news of salvation through Christ alone and he received my message. We then prayed that he would receive eternal life and the Holy Spirit of promise. When I looked up after our prayer, his face was radiating with God's light. It was as though I'd just seen and angel! I knew that God had just poured out the Holy Spirit upon him in great abundance! It was a sight to see. He thanked me profusely for coming to him. And we both shook hands and exchanged names. It seems that every time I go out to preach the gospel, God shows me a glimpse of His Holy Spirit at work. It is so very rewarding! I can't imagine doing anything else with my life! So we parted ways praising and rejoicing in the Spirit of Christ Jesus!

26 People Come of Christ Jesus At Seal Beach In One Afternoon

I went out to do evangelism at Seal Beach with my friend Brain Aschbrenner and a record number of 26 people received Jesus Christ as their Lord and Savior. Their names are Ann, Vanessa, Christian, Brandon, Angel, Vanessa, Vi, Pablo, Robert, Ashley, Josh, Arena, Audrey, Jerry, a group of five (I can't remember all their names), another group of five (I can't remember all of their names), Eric and Rebecca. When we came to Ann, I gave her a "God Loves You" card and read John 3:16-18 to her and then preached the gospel. She was Asian and didn't seem to ever have heard it before. But she enthusiastically embraced our message and prayed with us to repent of her sin and accept Jesus Christ into her life to be her Lord and Savior. Just then, after she'd prayed, it was as though the heavens opened up, as they'd done for Jesus Christ on the Mount of Transfiguration, and I was given the ability to see what was going on. Clouds, filled with glory descended upon us and made us exceedingly joyful. We left Ann and her daughter praising God for his good work. Then, on the beach, I timidly went up to a group of eight men and handed out "Are You Going To Heaven?" tracts, as we'd run out of the 50 "God Loves You" cards that we'd brought. The Spirit came upon me and I proclaimed the good news in power to the group. Then five of them came forward and said they wanted to make Jesus Christ the Lord and Savior of their lives! We all prayed together and I gave them each a Bible and list of churches to attend which they readily accepted! It was a great harvest. Then, Brian went up to a group of six and led five of them to the Lord Jesus Christ. It was incredible. Never before have I seen God harvest in this way. Praise be the Living God!

Another Seven Students Come To The LORD At Mission Viejo High School

I went out to Mission Viejo High School and shared the gospel using the "Are You Going To Heaven?" gospel tract and seven students received Christ! Their names are Frankie, Scott, Sierra, Ricci, John, Dan, and Ryan. When I saw John, Dan and Ryan coming up, I prayed, "God, please save them!" Then, I handed them out the tract. John promptly said, "I'm not into this! This is not for me!" But, then I said, "Just let me read something to you." So I went through the tract with them. Then the Holy Spirit's weight of conviction fell upon all of them and they all said they wanted to make Jesus Christ the Lord and Savior of their lives! John was so excited, he was literally beaming – a big change from a couple of minutes earlier! They all prayed with me to renounce their sins and accept Christ who is eternal life! It was a blessed interchange. And I praise God, who is the changer of hearts! We departed with handshakes and high-fives!